Be Daring. Be Different.

Reverse engineering of life. From who you are to who you want to be.

Christer Johnsen

Copyright © 2023 by Christer Johnsen

All rights reserved.

Published by Next Page Publishing Inc.

No portion of this book may be reproduced in any form without written permission from the publisher or author, except as permitted by U.S. copyright law.

This publication is designed to provide accurate and authoritative information in regard to the subject matter covered. It is sold with the understanding that neither the author nor the publisher is engaged in rendering legal, investment, accounting or other professional services. While the publisher and author have used their best efforts in preparing this book, they make no representations or warranties with respect to the accuracy or completeness of the contents of this book and specifically disclaim any implied warranties of merchantability or fitness for a particular purpose. No warranty may be created or extended by sales representatives or written sales materials. The advice and strategies contained herein may not be suitable for your situation. You should consult with a professional when appropriate. Neither the publisher nor the author shall be liable for any loss of profit or any other commercial damages, including but not limited to special, incidental, consequential, personal, or other damages.

Book Cover art image by Lars Løken

Illustrations by Larissa Soehn

Paperback ISBN: 978-1-7778600-8-0
eBook ISBN: 978-1-7778600-9-7

Contents

1. Introduction — 1
2. Purpose of this Book — 9
3. Who Am I? — 12
4. What is the Purpose of Life? — 29
5. Our Mind — 35
6. The Mind's Higher Faculties — 53
7. Quantum Physics and Energy — 69
8. Seven Laws of The Universe You Can Use to Live the Life You Really Want. — 73
9. Self-Image — 99
10. Set Goals — 108
11. How Do I Get There? Be Daring. Be Different. — 113
12. How To Do It: Create a Daily Ritual — 131
13. Summary — 135

14. Work With Me	137
Template for Your Daily Ritual	139
Daily Ritual Form	140
Acknowledgements	144
Author Bio	145

Chapter One

Introduction

"Who the fuck do you think you are?"

That was a default thought I had. Young, ambitious, highly educated, and in the start of a great career, I worked 24/7 and travelled internationally every week using my talent and my potential as a twenty-nine-years-young CEO. I'll admit, those who hired me had guts. But they did not regret it, I made sure of that. By the time I was thirty-four-years-old, I was in charge of an international group operating in more than thirty countries. I ran the show and took orders from no one. I was in control. I had it all; money, status, and power.

And yet I was deeply unhappy. Not the kind of unhappy you feel when something doesn't go your way. The kind of unhappy you feel when you know in your core that this isn't where you are meant to be.

It sounds so cliché. The man who has it all is constantly insecure, always doubting his next move, questioning everything he is doing while putting on the face of unwavering confidence. "I've got this," I would tell myself, more of a demand than a reassurance. My stomach would twist and knot as if I were in physical danger and my body was ready to fight or fly. It hurt. Physically and emotionally it hurt, but I always shoved it away. Ignored the warning signs that my body was so blatantly trying to give me. I was on a mission I thought was what I wanted.

This deep-rooted insecurity showed up most often as indignant anger. It reared up the most when people disagreed with me, or when someone made plans for my time without involving me. In those moments, my immediate thought was "Who the fuck do you think you are to do that to me?"

Even with all this deep-seated rage, I used my aggression to create great results for the companies I was in charge of. I was very competitive. But then one day, I started to change. Not surprisingly, this shift began when I was forty... Have you heard about the forty-years-old crisis? You know, the classic mid-life crisis that has sensible people do insensible things? I was all over it. Cars, watches, boats, motorcycles, leading the local swim club, volunteer activities day and night, and becoming a member of city council. Take all that and mix it with the pressures of my job, and you won't be surprised when I tell you that I ended up in hospital with my blood pressure through the roof and an uncontrollable nosebleed.

Those warning signs that my body gave me, the ones I pushed away? Well, they came back—and hit me like a truck.

"Who the fuck do you think you are to tell me that I HAVE to stay here overnight? I do NOT have time for this!" This one thought raged in my head as the hospital ER nurse checked my blood pressure. But something about this rage was different. I couldn't just push it away and demand control. No, my mind wasn't in control, my body was—and my body said, "Stay." And, for once, I did. I have always said there is a fine line between being stubborn and stupid. This time, when I chose to listen to my body, something started to change inside me.

Lying in the hospital bed I remembered being at scout camp when I was thirteen-years-old, already on the path of leadership as a young patrol leader. Our camp was at a small island far out in the archipelago of Southern Norway. For one week, far away from other people, we caught and cooked our own food, although the leaders had bread and butter in case we did not get any fish. We had tents, but the weather was so nice we slept under clear skies. When I looked at the stars, I felt at home. Lounging back, my head was tipped to the sky, as I wondered what was on the other side of those stars? Now, with my head tipped up to the hospital ceiling, I found a door—closed by dozens of years of programming from external factors—was opening up again.

In that hospital bed, with beeping machines around me, my nose stuffed with bandages to stop the bleeding, and the constant reminder of the fact that I was no longer in charge, I realized I had to change.

Not just a little change, but the kind that shows what is on the other side of the stars. On the other side of everything that goes on around us. And I wondered "Who the fuck do you think you are, Christer?" It was time for me to find a new way of existing. I had always done things *my* way; I had always been headstrong. Now I felt a strong surge for a deeper meaning to life. To find out what I really wanted. A new way to be daring and different. Where I put myself in center, where I do what I feel is right for me, where I follow my heart and my intuition. Not only doing what I thought others expected me to.

On the other side of a divorce, "Who the fuck do you think you are?" struck again, but this time I dared to try something new. I dared to do something different and explore. I started to study quantum physics. My good friend, Tom the psychiatrist, asked me to listen to Dr Robert Anthony's audiobook, *The Secret of Deliberate Creation*, and introduced me to books about *Martinus Cosmology*, and Florence Littauer's, *Personality Plus*. I was fascinated by Stephen Hawking's work about quantum physics. Everything I read led me deeper and deeper into the world of quantum physics and everything I consumed left me thinking,

> WOW—if my thoughts are energy, I better start thinking about what I want.

Easier said than done, but practice makes results, and I discovered that the more I stopped responding with,

"Who the fuck do you think you are?" the more space was left for true reflection. The true ability to think differently, dream bigger, and be deeply honest with myself. With practice came revelation. I dug up and dusted off a dream I had long forgotten but never lost. A dream that I held onto despite spending years getting further and further away from it. I want to sail around the world. I grew up sailing with my parents, and had served a year in the Norwegian Coast Guard, so it was not too distant to think I could do that.

Looking back now, I realize my dream of sailing around the world was less about sailing, and more about leaving everything behind in search for freedom.

It was my need for a restart in life—to break free from all external expectations I had tried to live up to. To find the true me that made this dream. To get relief from the pressure, frustration, and anger I had inside.

I realized this when I thought about my visualization of this dream. When I visualized standing on the deck of my boat as I left home port, I felt such a feeling of relief and freedom; it was not about all the wonderful experiences I could have on such a trip. That mental picture of a new start took me through a lot of rough times—and I still love the feelings it gives me. Freedom is one of my soothing words and needs.

Through my study of quantum physics, I developed a strong wish that I had known this earlier in my life. I felt this overwhelming feeling that I should have known who I was, and why I am as I am. That need to know myself spilled over into the need-to-know others. *What drove them to act the way they did? Why did I feel pulled towards anger instead of reflection? What was it that was driving us to these thoughts and reactions?* Once I found the answers I was looking for, I was irritated that this wasn't common knowledge. *Why wasn't this old knowledge about temperaments and personalities included in our education and studies? How is something that is so essential to all performance and happiness being left out of the traditional learning system?* "Who the fuck am I?" became "Who am I and why am I like this?"

With the question shift came the realization of a true-life advantage. I was now in the spot of learning and understanding. I was daring and different in a new way. I began to question if there was another path to success. One that didn't involve competition and aggression. One that was based on the abundance of our world, not a world where we think we have to fight and win to have a good life.

The obvious answer is, "Yes, there is." The bigger question was how? *How do I shed my old beliefs? How do I act in a way that will actually serve me? How do I get what I truly want? How are other people getting what they want? How do I do that?*

Relentless in my search for answers, I asked myself these questions hundreds of times throughout my studies. Which led me to this book.

Chapter Two

Purpose of this Book

The purpose of this book is to show you exactly what you can do to create the life you really want. I know that can sound too good to be true, and it was to me too. I found it interesting to listen to all these ideas, but I did not buy into them 100%. I studied for many years—and over the years I realized that the more I accepted the ideas, practiced the ideas, and lived the ideas, the better I felt and the better my life was.

Some of the ideas in this book are very different from what we have learned in school. We have all been taught many important things in school, but there are also many things we have not been taught. This is why I share them here with you.

To save you from spending ten years doing the same studying, wondering, trying, and failing that I did, you can read this book. Within these pages, I introduce you to several topics that are relevant to understanding *what* to do and *why* to do it. This is a handbook on how you can create the life you really want. All the things I write about in this book are included in my mentoring programs. This is an introduction, a motivation, and a short-cut, all contained in one book. It is a powerful message that can change your life.

I explain personalities, so you can understand yourself and others better. I explain how the body and the mind work. I take you through the laws that govern the Universe, and thereby, our lives. I relate our lives to physics and energy, and I tell you the exact steps you need to do to get more out of your life. Step by step.

Some of the facts, ideas, and stories I tell in this book may be different from what you expect. Some say they are mind blowing. My mind is not blown away from them, and I am sure you find them as fascinating as I do. Take your time to read it over and over again until you become what I write about. There is a big difference between reading and studying. To change your life, I highly recommend you not only read this book, but study it.

At the end you will find a list of some of the books I have studied to get a deeper understanding of these subjects. If you choose to explore them, these resources will give you an even deeper understanding of the material I introduce you to here.

To get the life you really desire is not difficult. It starts with being daring, being different. If you accept that idea, you have come a long way already.

When you start to deliberately create your life, it feels like riding a surfboard. You find the wave, and you ride it. Then you find a new wave and ride that better, and then a new one, and a new one. There are always waves coming your way. The picture on the front cover illustrates this. I hung this painting by Norwegian painter, Lars Løken, in my office; it is the same picture all my clients see in our video calls.

Chapter Three

Who Am I?

Personalities: Who Are We? And Why Are We the Way We Are?

Things have been thought about before. There isn't a moment in human history where we weren't thinking. At every turn, we think our society is the most advanced, and full of new knowledge. It's all so exciting. Well, people were thinking before too, and they were not far behind us. I often think that we actually are far behind today, or what today could be. More about that later in the b ook.

About two-and-a-half-thousand years ago, Hippocrates described four basic temperaments. Florence Littauer uses the same temperaments in her *Personality Plus* concept. And I use them in my mentoring for two reasons:

1. They are two-and-a-half-thousand years old—they have proven the test of time.

2. They are easy to understand and practical to use every day. I use them to understand my clients, my family, my customers, etc.

Your personality is the foundation of your self-image, self-talk, and perception. It is, therefore, the basis of everything you do and have done, and through using this system to understand yourself and others, you make a shortcut to changing your life. It all starts with understanding and knowledge. The first and most important knowledge is to understand yourself.

Sanguine- Let us do it the FUN way!

"Let us do it the fun way"
-Sanguine

The Sanguine is a pleasure-seeking and sociable personality. Their basic desire is to have fun. Their emotional desires are attention, affection, approval, acceptance, and presence of people. They need all eyes on them and they do whatever it takes to get that. A Sanguine has a fantastic ability to talk about everything to everyone, anytime. And it is not so important to them if they have all facts checked because they are great storytellers with a strong sense of humor. They just love to make others laugh, even if those others think they make a fool out of themselves.

Sanguines' weaknesses are that they are disorganized, struggle to remember details, exaggerate, are not serious about anything, and they trust others too much.

We recognize a Sanguine by her colorful dresses, yellow hair and pink nails, or his Hawaiian shirt and red shorts. Typically, they are artists, salesmen, or in creative areas of business. You will very rarely find a Sanguine accountant.

A Sanguine gets depressed when life is not fun or no one likes them. A depressed Sanguine would even prefer negative attention to no attention. They can make a fool of themselves just to get eyes on them. They control their environment through charm, and love being likable. And when that does not work, they get lost.

Choleric- Let us do it my way!

"Let us do it my way"
-Choleric

Cholerics are all about being in control and in charge. Their basic desires are appreciation for achievements, opportunity for leadership, something to control, and to participate in family decisions.

The Choleric is the master of doing things. Any time spent being unproductive is considered a waste of time. Cleaning the house while talking on the phone, or watching a movie while doing dishes, or listening to a podcast while doing the lawn—no problem! Multitasking is the game of a Choleric. Others can see them as too bossy, domineering, arrogant, and insensitive.

Cholerics are great leaders. They see the big picture—able to move from the highest level to the smallest detail in seconds, they are very good at decision-making. In mere moments, they see what is right, make the decision, and move forward with the full expectation that everyone else will follow.

A Choleric gets depressed when life is out of control, and they are afraid of losing control of anything. Cholerics control their environment through anger (if you haven't guessed, I am a Choleric-Melancholy, made obvious by the constant thought, "Who the fuck do you think you are?") and they can achieve more than any other type. There is almost no limit to all the things a Choleric can do in a short time. Workaholics—that is their last name. They see themselves as productive and do not understand why others are not the same.

Melancholic- Let us do it the perfect way.

"Let us do it the perfect way"
-Melancholic

Melancholy is the puzzle maker, the watch-maker, the engineer. To them, all the bits and pieces have to fit together in life—and the goal is to have everything perfect. They are deep thinkers and can seem downcast from outside. But they are not. They are just living in their perfect internal world, where everything goes as planned.

A Melancholy seeks perfection in everything. This perfection is created in their thoughts. And if things do not go as planned, they make new plans. Or they already have four-to-five different plans to make sure they cover all possible outcomes before they start. They are experts in "What-If-Then-Else" planning. And of course, everything must be according to the rules and well-regulated at all costs. Vacation without a schedule is a no-go for a Melancholy; their round-Britain car trip is scheduled in Excel, taking into account Google Maps' average traffic information, and they have several alternative routes for every stage of the trip.

A Melancholy can ask you about the strangest small details, and the answer they are looking for is the last piece in the puzzle of their perfect plan. A strong Melancholy can sit in peace and quiet, then suddenly say, "Ok everybody. Let us do it like this." And everybody looks at her wondering what has happened now, what they are doing, and when they are doing what they do not know about? The Melancholy has had all conversations in her head and created the "perfect plan," not even realizing she held all the conversations in her head. If you live with a strong Melancholy, you may sometimes feel the need to have a Bluetooth connection to your partner's brain to be involved in the planning.

Melancholy is emotionally sensible; they need time to think, they need to talk, and they are good listeners. Long talks where they can explain what they think and how they see the world is very important to a Melancholy. They have a rich "internal world" and talking is a way for them to share that with others.

A Melancholy controls their environment through moods, and when you know them really well, you can see how they use emotions to manipulate their environment.

Where do you find Melancholy people? Everything that is related to law, order, and systems. If it has structure and rules, and perfection and logic are important, you will find a Melancholy there.

Phlegmatic- Let us do it – or maybe tomorrow.

"Let us do it... or maybe tomorrow"
-Phlegmatic

Peace of mind is the emotional need for a Phlegmatic. They are easy-going, stable, and dependable. They are not performance oriented. Goals are unnecessary and if you do not get things done today, you can do them tomorrow. If not today, maybe tomorrow, or maybe the day after tomorrow.

Phlegmatics hate to make decisions—a pure Phlegmatic cannot make a decision because choosing one thing means deciding not to do something else, and that might be emotionally challenging. A Phlegmatic can be seen as highly empathic and kind, but the true cause is the Phlegmatic's need for peace of mind, not their focus on others. If a decision might affect other people negatively, a Phlegmatic will not do it because it can take away his peace of mind.

A Phlegmatic is easy-going and always content. If a Choleric is seen as a workaholic, a Phlegmatic is the procrastinator. They never get things done because their main concern is peace of mind. To have a cup of tea and watch the same British crime series from 1992 for the sixth time—that is a great life to them. As for that growing pile of laundry, the Phlegmatic will think, "I can do that tomorrow."

Phlegmatics control their environment through procrastination. By choosing to do it later, they remain in control. This means that if you do get a committed decision from a Phlegmatic—well, do not get upset if they say they'll do that tomorrow. Despite this constant procrastination, there is a limit to a Phlegmatic's patience. When their line is crossed (which, admittedly, can take a long time) they burst out in anger—*Enough! Stop it!* And everyone around wonders, "Where did that come from?"

Phlegmatic people are most commonly found in service industries such as public services, schools, transportation, bookkeeping, auditing, and tax authorities. Places where they do not have to make decisions, can work without stress, and where they start at 9am and leave at 4pm.

Summary of Primary Personality

We all have a dominant type of temperament, and all personality types are present in all of us to various degrees. That degree can also change over time or through personal development, though the genetically-dominating personality is normally dominant throughout life. It can be difficult to pick one that is your dominant personality since we all see ourselves subjectively.

A good description of the primary personality can be this story from my life.

A woman I know rather well had a half-finished painted garden fence. It was like that for three years. To a Choleric, that would be impossible to have incomplete. To a Melancholy, it would be a disaster not to have it done right. To a Sanguine, it could be fun. A Phlegmatic does not care what others think; they can do it tomorrow.

We are all a mix of all four personalities, but many have a clear dominating type and a clear number two. I am a Choleric with Melancholy as second. I like to be in control, I am a good decision-maker, and I like to have things in system. I like to do my yearly tax report, I do my own accounting, and I often make to-do lists and routines for myself.

Personalities and Relationships

You might wonder why your partner, boss, or the employees you have hired are the way they are? We can compare the attraction of personalities with yin and yang. We attract others that fill our own gaps. A Melancholy likes the "livingness" of Sanguine. A Phlegmatic likes the control and decision-making abilities of a Choleric. A Sanguine likes the order of a Melancholy. A Choleric likes to control a Phlegmatic. Unless we are aware of this, it is very easy to choose and attract what we like—and not what we need. This point is essential in all partnerships, whether it is a marriage or a professional relationship.

At the beginning of a relationship the differences are highly valued, but over time we tend to want to change the other person(s) to be more like us, which is not a route to success. Through reflection and analysis of this chapter, you can begin to better understand yourself and others—and value the differences instead of trying to change others. It is more challenging but much more rewarding; it is easier to love when we understand.

Summary of the Four Personalities

These two tables summarize the core of the four personalities. The arrows in the middle of the first figure illustrate the natural attraction between the personalities.

PLAYFUL SANGUINE	LEAD Extroverted - Optimistic - Outspoken	POWERFUL CHOLERIC
Basic Desire: Have Fun **Emotional Needs** Attention Affection Approval Acceptance **Controls with:** Charm		**Basic Desire:** Have Control **Emotional Needs** Loyalty Sense of Control Appreciation Credit for Work **Controls with:** Anger
PLAY Witty - Easy-going - Not Goal Oriented	✕	**WORK** Decisive - Organized - Goal Oriented
PEACEFUL PHLEGMATIC **Basic Desire:** Have Peace **Emotional Needs** Peace and Quiet Feeling of Worth Lack of Stress Respect **Controls with:** Procrastination	ANALYZE Introverted - Pessimistic - Soft-spoken	**PERFECT MELANCHOLY** **Basic Desire:** Have Perfection **Emotional Needs** Sensitivity Support Space Silence **Controls with:** Moods

Personality Profiles

PLAYFUL SANGUINE

Strengths
People Person
Humor
Creative and Colorful
Great Storyteller

Weaknesses
Disorganized
Talks Too Much
Easily Distracted
Often Late

POWERFUL CHOLERIC

Strengths
Decisive
Works Well Under Pressure
Production-Oriented
Great Leader

Weaknesses
Too Opinionated
Workaholic
Overly Intense
Insensitive

PEACEFUL PHLEGMATIC

Strengths
Adaptable
Good Under Pressure
Good Listener
Kind

Weaknesses
Too Quiet
Procrastinator
Stubborn
Avoids Conflict

PERFECT MELANCHOLY

Strengths
Attention to Detail
Good with Numbers
Great at Process/Systems
Self-Starter/ Initiative

Weaknesses
Lacks Spontaneity
Struggles Under Pressure
Hard to Please
Can't Function Without Structure

Action Steps

Discuss the different personalities with someone who knows you well—and who you know well. Maybe your partner or a colleague. With an open, neutral mind, explore which personalities you think you have as primary and secondary?

You can also try to look at yourself from a neutral perspective. Think about what is important to you, and what do you really like and dislike?

In my mentoring programs, we use one of many *Personality Plus* tests available online. These tests are based on Florence Littauer's books.

Chapter Four

What is the Purpose of Life?

You might be thinking, "What a silly question." Or maybe you are wondering the same thing yourself. Or maybe you're thinking, "Christer, who the fuck do you think you are to think such a mind-blowing thought?" Life is life, right? Or is there more to it? Whether you are on the "What kind of question is that?" or, "I have the same question," side of things, let me tell you what I think life is. Because I believe there is more to it than what most of us think and have thought.

Are we simply animals with an advanced brain, or are we something more? A friend of mine who hunts once told me that a moose's brain is the size of a tennis ball.

No wonder their life is all about survival, food, and the strongest one "gets lucky" once a year. Our brain is much more advanced and we have some mental abilities that animals do not have. Yet animals are always perfect in their environment, while many humans do not feel comfortable in their environments at all. Why is it like that?

When we look at today's society, it seems the purpose of life is to become loyal taxpayers. We are parts of the big machinery of society; as soon as we enter kindergarten (in Norway kids start at one-year-old), we are taught that the only way to a good and secure life is to be a part of the system. To be loyal to the school system. Read the books we are supposed to read. Play the sports that our parents want to mirror themselves in. Finish, at least, a bachelor's degree from college. Get a job and start to pay down that all-too-large study loan that the State so willingly "gave" us. Oh, and don't forget about saving money because we might want to retire some day.

Most importantly, we shall not dream, and we shall not create our own future. Most kids are efficiently programmed to be a part of the system—not to be daring, different, and creative humans.

The truth we know, the one we are taught in such an early stage of life, is the one told in the media. It comes from the unwavering trust we are supposed to have in the politicians and bureaucrats—because they know best. And maybe they do. Maybe that is the best way to get everyone at a certain level of Maslow's pyramid. Of course, this all differs with country and culture. But in general, we see a more and more mechanically-organized society where everything is controlled and arranged.

But the question becomes:

> Is there more to this life than this daily routine that we are all so brainwashed and conditioned to fall into? The one that comes with existing as part of an organized society? Are we slaves of what others tell us we shall think; are we bound to perform daily trivia—or is there more to this life?

If the question of, "What is the purpose of life?" feels too large for you to handle or process, think about these questions:

1. Is the Universe focused on scarcity or abundance?

2. Do we need to work hard to get what we want in

life?

3. How would life be if we could create our own reality?

4. How would you feel if you could create your own circumstances and live the life you dream about?

5. Why do some people have so much life while others have so little?

6. Why are some happy with little while others always strive for more?

7. How far can I go?

8. How many can I help?

9. How much fun can I have?

10. How good can I feel?

For sure, the personality types have an influence here—but there is more to it than that.

I see us humans as more than advanced animals. I see us as energetic beings living in a physical body. We live in a world created by energy, so why would we expect ourselves

BE DARING. BE DIFFERENT.

to be anything but abundant and magnetic forms of energy. Some call it "soul," others call it the "essential silent partner," others call it "spiritual being." I think of humans as souls that have lived many lives, and that our job in this life is to realize that we are not bound to a certain way of life. That our society does not dictate our happiness. The soul we hold in our bodies is eternal and we need to honor it by creating our own life by working *with* our thoughts, not against them. We can create our own environment, our own life. We are catalysts who can change the energy that surrounds and consumes us. We can control the way we feel and, thereby, how we affect other people. And through that, we can create the life we really desire.

> Life is lived in contrast. We must know what it is to be cold and to be warm. We must have darkness to see light. We must feel sadness to enjoy happiness. We must know what feeling bad is to know what feeling good is.

Our feelings are a guiding system which show us the right way. This feels bad and makes you unhappy—then it is wrong for you. This feels great and it is so effortless—then you are on the right track.

To me, the purpose of life is its "livingness." It is to see how far I can go in this life. My goal is to help as many people as possible see how fantastic life can be when we live it forwards instead of backwards. We live life backwards when we believe that it is everything around us that creates our life. We live life forward when we think about and focus on what we really want and thereby create our own life.

Action Steps

Write down a list of all the contrasts you see in your life today. Things you really like, and things you really do not like.

How do you want to live? What is your dream life like?

How do you NOT want to live?

What do you like to do? What is your dream job or dream activity?

What do you like not to do?

What is important to you in your life? For instance: freedom, having order, attention, or peace of mind (that is related to your personality).

Chapter Five

Our Mind

No one has ever seen the mind. We have seen the body with a head. We know what the brain looks like because someone has opened the scalp on a (hopefully) dead person. But the brain is the least understood organ in the body. It is this grey mass, full of energy and thoughts, that is linked to a fantastic nervous system. To me, the nervous system looks like an electrical system with constantly firing neurons and pathways being carved to form habits and routines—it is an overly complicated and beautiful circuit board of energy. Nerve pulses are electrical signals where the physical nerves are high speed cables connected in a central hub system. Every little surge results in thought or action.

Sometimes when I see this picture, I think, "If you are looking for an alien (Extraterrestrial life), look in the mirror." Looking at this, I know we are too full of wonders to have been created by accidental evolution. It is just too undiscovered, and too magic.

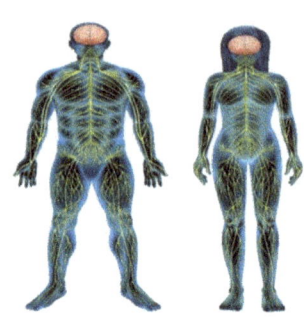
Photo: Colourbox.com

What about the mind then? The center of our thoughts, beliefs, and feelings. Not the systematically firing neurons, but the part of us left unseen. The views we hold, the judgements we make, and the dreams we aspire to achieve. How does the mind work, and can we make it work for us? Can we truly control our minds?

In our culture we are taught NOT to use the mind in the best way for us. We live in a mechanical age where we base almost everything on the perfectly rational human—Homo economicus, is it called.

Despite where I am now and the beliefs that I hold, I have studied enough economics to know that we are not rational. I know rational. I know what it is supposed to look like. My master's degree in business and economics ensures that. But I have also worked a lot with marketing—and all marketers know that it is all about emotions. If you are not convinced, let me give you an example I use with most of my clients:

When you found your partner, did you create a table with five-to-seven candidates in rows, and fifteen-to-twenty different criteria on the things that are most important to you. Did you rank each criteria based on objective results, then give each candidate a score from zero-to-ten on each criteria? Did you finally add every column and choose the one with the highest score? That is how a rational human would do this. (If you did, I am pretty sure you are a very strong Melancholy personality.) Or did you look at those beautiful eyes, that smile, and think, "Hmm, this could be interesting. I want to try that one out."

Right. I am 99.9% sure that most of us did not make that table. In 2017, Richard Thaler got a Nobel Prize in economics for his idea that humans are not rational in their economical behavior. It is great to see that the world is evolving in what I think is the right direction and moving away from the supposed rationality to see us as more highly emotional beings.

We are all controlled by our emotions. We typically react first, analyze later. This is called post-rationalizing: "I responded that way because he pissed me off." "I cried because my life is hard."

My dad always says that everything expensive he buys is a good investment. He knows nothing about Internal Rate of Return or Net Present Value, payback time or cash flow (he is a landscape architect). He does not know much about money either. But he knows a lot about the feelings those purchases give him. That is what matters to him. He knows a lot about the feelings and interactions the beautiful cities, parks, and highway stops he designed give a lot of people. The most important thing in life is how you feel at this moment.

> Because life is lived in this moment through your emotions and feelings. Life is not lived one hour ago. It is not lived tomorrow. It is lived here and now.

And life is all about how you feel now, *in this moment*. Contrasts are created in your feelings, and in these contrasts, you live your life.

What is this "mind thing" that is so abstract that we cannot see it? This mind we live in and with, every second of our life, even when we are asleep, sick, or playing sports?

Many books about psychology describe that our physical senses are for survival and that we use our bodies to bring the next generation life. I agree that we use our physical senses to do that too. But there is more to them than that—so much more.

The brain and the nervous system are the thinking and sensing organs of the body. Thoughts and ideas are created in the brain and felt and experienced in the body. We have five physical senses—see, hear, taste, touch, smell—that give us the ability to perceive and experience the physical part of life. The purpose of those five senses is to give us physical experiences in the form of contrasts so we can experience life. They are not made for *creating* our life. They are made for giving us experience of the life *we create*.

A few pages earlier I wrote, "We live in a world created by energy, and we are energetic beings." Maybe you thought, "Wow—he is out there." Let me give you a few insights.

We have more energy in our body than in a bolt of lightning.

Read that again.

We have more energy in our body than in a bolt of lightning.

A bolt of lightning is one billion volts. A human cell generates .07 volts of electricity. At 37.5 trillion cells, that's 2.625 trillion volts in a human body. Luckily it is not as concentrated or condensed, nor does it come out as a bolt of lightning from our body—that could be painful or devastating. Think about touching someone else and giving them one billion volts. That would be a relationship killer, literally.

We do not get our energy from "somewhere." We have all the energy we need inside us, in each and every cell. According to biologists Ron Sender and Ron Milo, we make 3.8 million new cells every second. You are a walking power plant creating your own energy all the time, as long as you put wood on the fire in the form of calories.

There must be some kind of control mechanism controlling this massive amount of energy—what is it? Better yet, what can we do with all this energy?

Your Thoughts Are Energy

If we put electrons on the scalp we can measure brain activity, which shows us that different thoughts are made in different parts of the brain. Scientists know that different thoughts have different frequencies or wavelengths. By definition, for something to have a frequency or wavelength, it must be composed of energy. It's energy riding those waves in our brains.

All thoughts we have create a sensation or feeling in our body through the nervous system. We think about something that scares us, and we feel the sensation of fear in the body. We think about something that makes us happy, and we feel the physical sensation of joy. It feels like different waves of energy going through our body. And it is undeniably energy.

We can measure it in heart rhythm and blood pressure. We can see the energy leaving the body through Kirlian photography, where the energy glows in different colors around the organ.[1] Most of us are aware of these sensations in our body. We can say that feelings are conscious awareness of this energy or vibration. *We perceive the energy as vibration because all energy has frequency and wavelength.*

Photo: Kirlian photograph of a fingertip, 1989
Wikipedia

All animals have a nervous system as described above but, as discussed before, we are not animals, we are something more. This is where we differ and this is the magical opportunity—if we use this the right way. You can, and should, be using this power plant of body and brain as a control mechanism to create your own world. A world where you live the life you want.

Early in the 1990s, Western doctors found out there are forty thousand brain cells in the heart. Did you know

---

1. Russian electrical engineer and his wife Valentina developed this photo technique that technically is a way of creating images of coronal discharges around an object.

about that? Scientists have said they think the heart is a more autonomous organ than they first thought. I mentioned this to a client of mine who is a Muslim, and he said, "I know – it is written in the Koran." I was amazed—*how did they know that more than seven hundred years ago?* This realization reminded me that there has been a lot of "thinking" in earlier ages too, and that thought humbles me. Our scientists have not discovered the purpose of these brain cells yet—because they are looking for something that can be measured scientifically. My first thought when my client told me about the Koran is that this is where our intuition is—in our heart. Intuition is our connection to the Universal forces, and our heart is our igniting power to all our energy. Everything is energy and we have the power to use it deliberately.

Reverse Engineering of Life

In addition to a thinking heart, all humans have six higher mental faculties. They are all unique to each of us and we can use them, and train them, to be better. They are:

1. Imagination

2. Perception

3. Will

4. Memory

5. Intuition

6. Reasoning

Before I jump into describing each of those further, I want to show you a model where we turn the rational human upside down. Where the mind is the essential part, and the body is an instrument for physical experiences and feelings—remember that feelings are conscious awareness of vibration. Your body actually vibrates, and that is because we are full of energy. I call this model *Reverse Engineering of Life*. We literally turn life upside down. Bob Proctor introduced me to this model—he called it the "Stick Person"—and it definitely turned my life upside down. It made me think, "Who the fuck do you think you are, Christer?" This was a true eye opener to me about how I can create the life I really want.

Conscious Mind- Thinking Mind

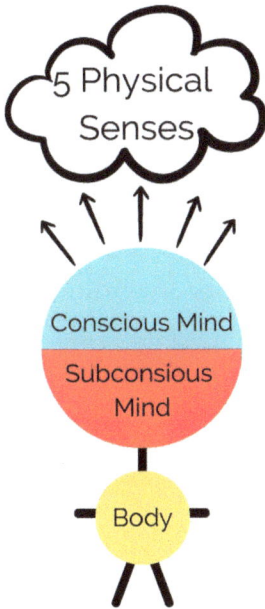

The top half of your mind is the conscious mind. This is where you think and reason, where you accept or reject ideas and thoughts. It is your intellect and where your physical senses are: see, hear, taste, touch, smell. It's also where your will is—it is here you decide what you want to do and to focus on.

> Most people live like this: they experience something around them, and that causes a feeling in them, and they react. They react on reflex. They are programmed.

Someone yells at me, and that annoys me, and therefore I am angry. Someone serves me a glass of water, and that makes me smile, and therefore I am happy. They are controlled by what happens around them and how they are used to reacting. How they perceive life is an effect of what happens around them. They give away the control of their lives, and they are not the *cause* of their own lives. Instead, their life is the effect of what happens around them. They do not deliberately choose how to think and act to create the life they really want. They are reacting instead of acting.

The conscious mind can accept or reject any idea. This is where you choose what is true or not. No person or circumstance can force you to think any thoughts you do not want.

> This is important because the thoughts you choose to think about—whether the start of the thought is something happening around you, or the thought comes from your own inspiration—will eventually determine your results in life.

Your thoughts are created from the ideas you accept, and as you accept an idea, it is impressed upon your subconscious mind. You give the idea permission to live inside your mind and body as thoughts. You give it the power to exist as it is, however harmful or helpful it might be.

Subconscious Mind- Conditioned Mind

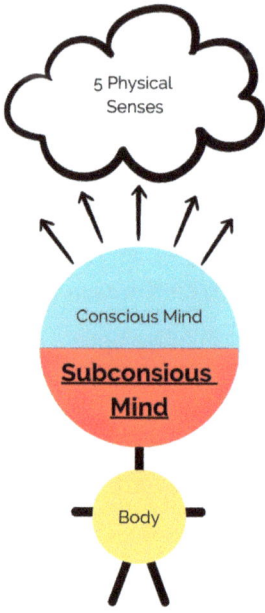

In the image, it might look like your mind is your head or the brain. But that is not how it is. The mind is this abstract thing that exists without being seen physically. Your entire mind functions in every cell of your body.

Every thought or word your conscious mind chooses to accept (whether it's currently true or not), the subconscious mind must accept. It has no ability to reject. An example of this is a dream; when you dream it is real to you. You feel it in the body and it gives you emotions.

This part of your mind knows no limits. Everything is possible, and it does not choose false or true. It accepts. So everything you put in here (and yes, by accepting it, you are choosing to put it into your subconscious mind) will affect your feelings. Ultimately, you can choose how you feel by controlling your thoughts.

Any thought you consciously impress over and over upon the subconscious becomes fixed in there. The thoughts become programs in our mind—habits. These habits automatically express themselves in feelings and actions, conditioned responses that exist forever or until they are replaced. By controlling your thoughts, you can reprogram your mind to new habits. *Physically, new neural pathways are created in your body.*

CHRISTER JOHNSEN

Your Body Is an Instrument for the Mind

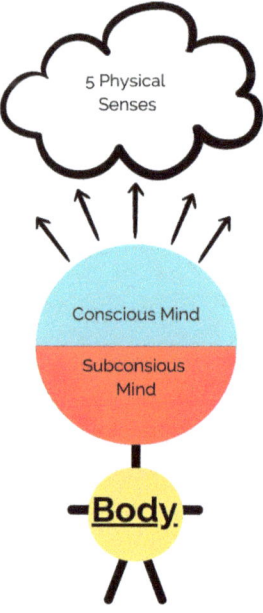

Your body is the physical representation of you. It is your instrument to experience the physical world. You want, and need, to learn how to play this instrument as a true professional—to be the best in the world to create the life you really want .

The ideas, thoughts, or images that you consciously choose and impress upon the subconscious move your body into action. The actions you take determine the results you get in life.

What you think affects how you feel. How you feel affects your actions. And your actions create the results. The result is the life you live.

It is equally that simple and that hard to understand—because through our entire life we have been taught to be rational. That is wrong. We are emotional powerplants who can use our body to create the life we really want. And what you want is only up to you.

Your emotions can control your relationship with situations. By controlling your thoughts, you get the horse in front of the cart, you use your ideas and thoughts to create the life you want. You have never been on the wrong path—you have just walked it backward. When you understand this and *accept that idea*—a new dimension opens up for you. *When we accept this idea, a new door opens,* and we suddenly have the ability to use our higher mental faculties to manage our thoughts and create the life we really want.

Action Steps

1. Write down the first thoughts you think every morning.

2. Reflect on how your thoughts influence your feelings.

3. Write down the one thought that makes you feel the best.

4. Write down all the fears you have and how they are impacting you/the power they hold over you. Write what will happen to you if they occur.

Chapter Six

The Mind's Higher Faculties

Our personality is the basis of all we are and all we do. It is the basis of our life as we know it, the thing that governs our actions, behaviors, and beliefs. To change something as significant as our life we must start with understanding our personality, and then we can understand and train our higher faculties to become a better version of ourselves. Through understanding our mind, and how we can control our thinking, we can grow the personality sides of us that are necessary to create the life we want.

A client of mine had a goal of starting up his own business. At that time, he was a clear Phlegmatic with Melancholy as second, and Choleric as a weak third. He had worked on his business plan for several years, but never came out of the starting blocks and launched the business. To be an entrepreneur, you need to make decisions and to put your plans into action. Through my mentoring we developed his business skills by developing the Choleric sides of him. He now understands that "procrastination" is his first response as a Phlegmatic, and "overthinking and planning" is his second response as Melancholy. He is consciously aware of this, so he challenges himself to be Choleric and make quick decisions. Today, he owns a very successful business.

Imagination

Our imagination is our ability to create fantasies. To see the invisible. The daydream. Bob Proctor said "Imagi**NA-TION** is the greatest nation in the world!" It is so true. We can build anything, go anywhere, and be anyone in our fantasies and imagination. There are no limits—except our own thoughts about what is acceptable to dream about. Those limitations are only created by our self-image.

Our self-image is what we think we can do, and what we think we can not do. It is our self- talk. It is the picture of our selves. Do you see yourself as successful or not? Do you see yourself as a good parent? Are you a good driver? Are you good with other people? Are you a world class author? Or do you talk yourself down and think that you are not good enough to get what you really want?

Imagination is a mental muscle that you train to use. Children flex this muscle daily. It truly knows no bounds as it takes shape from the movies and books we consume, the stories told by our friends, the conversations we overhear, but don't fully understand. As we grow, we start to put limitations on this imagination. We begin to make assumptions about what it must be or what it should be. We stop letting ourselves be lost to potential, instead we get pulled into the reality we think must exist.

If you were, for a moment, to paint a picture inside your head of how you really want to live, what you really want to do, who you really want to be—would you be able to see it clearly? Could you use your imagination to create the life you dream about? As Andrew Carnegie said, "Any idea that is <u>held</u> in the mind, that is <u>emphasized</u>, that is either feared or revered, will immediately start to clothe itself in the most appropriate form available." The first time I read that, my thought was, "I should rather think about what I want—and not what I do not want."

That is where most people go wrong. They use their imagination to create what they do not want because they are more focused on what they do not want than what they want. That is the biggest mistake you can make in life.

When I want to "twist my mind" and think out of the box, I use my imagination to think how others would see what I am thinking about. I often use one of my mentors as my "imagination partner" and see things how I think the world is through their eyes. To me, that is a great way of extending my own imagination and is a great exercise to do with many topics.

Intuition

I think we have all heard about intuition. Or perhaps more about people we see as intuitive. Many of them are seen as spiritual. But you do not have to be intuitive to be spiritual, or vice versa. Intuition is, just like the other five higher faculties, a mental muscle you can train to trust. It is closely related to your ability to make decisions. Intuition is in your heart—it is a silent voice that tells you what to do.

When I go hiking, sailing, and diving, I feel myself surrender to my intuitive side. I think this occurs because I calm down my external sensors and am at one with nature.

I listen with my heart, follow my heart, let nature talk to me, and allow magic to flow. The kind of magic that brings stillness to life. Like not wanting to break eye contact with a flock of grouse looking at me from five feet away, while the shallow breath I dare to take catches in my throat. Or hiking in Norway with my kids when a reindeer and her two calves passed less than ten meters from the river where we were drinking fresh water. Or when I sense the wind before the gusts come to take my boat from a slow glide to a full speed race. These senses, the feeling of being a part of something bigger, like you exist in harmony with everything around you, are the moments when your intuition is screaming at you. It's your job to listen.

To trust your intuition in daily life can be more difficult. *It takes more practice.* There is so much noise around us all the time and we are so well trained not to listen to it. We are trained to be rational. I actually needed a painful experience to start to listen to my intuition in my daily life. Some years ago while doing the dishes, as I put a big knife on a magnetic strip I thought, "If it drops, I cannot catch it." It fell—and at the expense of my fingers, I caught it. At first I screamed—then I laughed—and my wife looked like a living question mark. Nope, I do not like pain—but

I realized that this was a gift and a reminder to always listen to my intuition. I needed that emotional impact to change.

I needed the awakening to become more aware of my intuition in daily life. And to practice every day to listen to it when it talks to me. Because intuition is like someone whispering to you while the rest of the world screams at you. It is subtle, and it is important. On a spiritual level, we can say that intuition is your connection to your heart and soul.

When you have strengthened your ability to listen to your intuition, it is a wonderful "silent guide" to have in decision making. In business we call it "gut feeling"—we just know that we know that it is right to do, even if logic says something else. When that feeling is there, I do what it says—even though it sometimes seems illogical.

Steve Jobs said, "Have the courage to follow your heart and intuition. They somehow already know what you truly want to become. Everything else is secondary." I fully agree. And I think there is more to it. I think heart and intuition is one, that the purpose of the forty thousand brain cells in our hearts is to be our intuition. That is where our intuition is. "As a man thinketh in his heart, so is he" the Bible says (Proverbs 23:7).[1] And I agree. It is all about our heart and feelings.

Will.

You can use your will in many ways. One way is physical—do fifty pushups in one minute or run a marathon. I have only run a half-marathon, so I do not know exactly what I am talking about here, but I am pretty sure the full forty-two kilometers takes a lot more willpower than my half-marathon.

The second version of will is your thoughts. You can also use your will to control your thoughts.

I say that again.

You can also use your will to control your thoughts.

Remember—we become what we think about. Read again the quote from Andrew Carnegie: "Any idea that is held in the mind, that is emphasized, that is either feared or revered, will immediately start to clothe itself in the most appropriate form available."

As a mental faculty, the will is closely related to what we want. I often compare it with a compass. A normal

---

1. Author inspired by James Allan's As A Man Thinketh

compass always points the red arrow to North. Your will is a compass that always points your thoughts to what you want—if you use it the right way. Remember Carnegie said, "any idea that is held in the mind... [and] emphasized." Your mental faculty will always direct you to the thought that is held in the mind; that is your dominant thought throughout the day and it is either feared or revered. That is why we say, "Think about what you want, not what you do not want." And when you think about what you do not want, use your will to change your thoughts to what you do want.

When I started my process of deliberately creating my life, I used my imagination to create a picture of me sailing out from my home port. That thought made me feel so good. Every time I experienced something that made me feel bad—or I had a bad thought myself—I used my will to change from the bad thought to the thought and picture of me sailing. My goal became my dominant feeling of the day. I held that idea in my mind because I really wanted it to happen.

With our mental will, we focus on our goals—what we really want. We will all other thoughts and impressions away from our mind. Our will gives us focus on what we want. Focus is energy that gives life to the beautiful painting you have made with your imagination. This is where you say, "This I will do, no matter what." This is where you say, "I never, never, never give up." Because I want to do this. Because I want it. And that is the only argument you need for having a goal.

Memory

In their *Magic in your Mind* program, Bob Proctor, Mary Morrisey, and Sandy Gallagher tell a story about a fairytale princess who rejected the idea that memory can only be used backwards, because she thought that was dull. "Why don't you use the memory forwards instead?" she asked. That is a great idea! One of my mentoring clients told me he made a future diary describing himself in his vision of his goal. He described his path on his way to the goal, including all details of when it was and how it felt when he experienced the goal. I really liked that idea, so I started to do the same thing. I started to build future memories.

You can train your memory to remember whatever you want. The first step is to stop telling yourself that you are bad at remembering. I told myself I was bad at remembering names—and I believed it until the day a colleague of mine said that I always remembered names. I realized I was good at something I thought I was bad at.

The second step to train your memory is to understand how it works. The memory remembers extremes and pictures. We do not remember letters or words—we remember the pictures the letters and words create. And the stranger or more extreme pictures and stories we create, the easier they are to remember, because our memories will stand out from our daily trivia and be something fun to recall.

There are thousands of books and videos about how to further train our memory, so I will not go into details here. What is important for me is that memory is a mental muscle that can be trained and used to our advantage. And we can use it to remember how to use the mind to create the life we want.

Reasoning

The simple explanation is that this is your ability to think. This may be the most important faculty because this is where your thoughts are created from the ideas you accept. You combine logical and illogical thoughts and ideas to create strengths of thoughts. Illogical thoughts are important in all true creation—because to create that which we have not thought before, we have to think beyond what has been thought before. We have to think outside our own box of ideas and automatic thoughts. Sources of illogical thoughts can be our imagination and our intuition.

It is in your reasoning faculty that you describe what, for you, is true or not true. It is where you make conclusions based on the facts in your mind and where you hold your judgments. Since perception is individual, what you consider true and fact is a choice you make, and that is a foundation for your thinking.

Bob Proctor said that maybe three percent of people can effectively use their reasoning faculty to create the life they want. I am not sure this figure is correct. One of the reasons I wrote this book is because I have a burning desire that we multiply that number—and that is a lot of people when there are eight billion people in the world.

You use your reasoning to think about what you want. And from there you create the life you want. If your will is your compass, then reasoning is your map that shows the playing field and possible routes to your goal—based on your awareness today. That is very important because we do not want to live like a fly that tries to go through a closed window and never sees the open door two feet away. More of the same gives you more of the same. By using your reasoning to think about what you want, you can create a new map and new routes—if you are one of the three-or-more percent who are willing to try it.

Perception

Is your blue my blue? We were taught colors by someone pointing at something blue saying "blue." But do you see the same blue as me—or is your blue different? It is different because perception is subjective. Can you imagine that there are eight billion different perceptions in this world? That thought is amazing to me. It is mind blowing. So, my world is not your world. We all live in our own world, with our own thinking, and we create our own reality—because you see it differently from me.

That we all have different perceptions is not a new discovery. Plato described this almost two-and-a-half-thousand years ago in his *Cave Theory* where the man in the cave thinks he perceives the true world. But when viewed from outside, what he sees are only the shadows of the true world outside the cave. The shadows are created from the sun outside in the true world. Thus, our perception is derived from our ideas of the world, not from the true world.

Perception is closely linked to personality. It is closely linked to education and programming. And it is closely linked to awareness. A client of mine who is an electrical engineer said, "Christer, I cannot tell my colleagues what we talk about. They will think I have turned mad." And that is strange to me—because it is all physics and laws. But we think that the Universal laws do not apply to us.

When the Wright brothers were the first in the world to fly a machine, their critics said that they only flew for fourteen seconds. The Wrights smiled and said, "We kept it there for fourteen seconds." That was their perception.

Perception is reality. It is your reality. You own your reality—and you can use this to your advantage.

What you perceive as a loss, or as a negative, can be positive for the person next to you. It is your choice to perceive a thing as good or bad: "I am so happy that this lovely date dumped me because I know that someone much better is waiting for me."

To be neutral to what happens around you can open your perception and make it possible for you to change what you think, how you react, what you perceive, and how your life is.

Let me share a story with you as told by a good friend of mine. Some hundred years ago, at the time when Spanish ships discovered America, there was a native tribe that lived on the prairie during winter and moved down to the sea during summer. They had lived like this, close to nature, for many generations. They were a part of nature. One day, there was a shift in the energy in the tipi village and everyone became restless; there was something different, something they had not experienced before. The sound of the wind was different, the waves were different, the air felt different. The warriors ran to the beach but they could not see or find anything different. They could not see what it was, but their intuition told them there was something wrong. And they trusted their intuition.

They gathered the tribal council who decided to call for the eldest medicine man. He asked everyone to calm down and continue their daily tasks. Then he went down to the beach, sat down, closed his eyes, stilled his mind, and cleared his perception—then opened his eyes and saw what the others had not been able to see because they were limited by their perception. He saw the armada of Spanish ships—something he had never seen before and did not understand—but he saw it and understood it could be a threat. That saved this tribe because he opened up his perception to what was unknown to him.

It was a deliberate choice for the medicine man to open his perception to see what was outside his box, outside his known world. He used his higher faculties wisely and changed the life of the tribe. You can do the same thing—you can change your life if you really want to.

Derived from this story we can ask ourselves:

Do I see it when I believe it?

Or do I believe it when I see it?

The truth will always resonate with you. It will feel good. Trust that feeling.

Action Steps

1. Write down the things that often happen around you that affect your feelings negatively. For instance, at work, at home, in traffic, or in a store. If the list is long, make a "Top 10" list.

2. Write down all the thoughts you have that make you feel great, energized, and full of spirit.

3. Take the first list, tear it into pieces, and throw it away. Stop thinking about it!

4. Keep the last list and think about all those things—every day. And continue to build the list longer and longer.

Chapter Seven

Quantum Physics and Energy

I really like the TV show *Big Bang Theory,* and watched it with our kids for years. I think we all can relate to some of those characters; a colleague once gave me a Sheldon figure, so I guess I am a little bit of him. Maybe not on the 3D-chess level of nerdiness, but I like some of the principles of quantum physics and, to me, this is the rational proof that I was looking for many years ago when I was introduced to the idea that we can create the life we really want.

We know that our body is a power plant, and that our thoughts are energy. We also know that there is a cause-and-effect relation that always works. If you do something it affects something, however small it is. If you kick a ball, you give it moving energy and it will move until the energy from friction stops it.

There is no simple definition to what energy is. The US Energy and Information Administration writes, "Energy is defined as the ability to do work, which is the ability to exert a force causing displacement of an object." Despite this confusing definition, its meaning is very simple: energy is just the force that causes things to move.

Right—but what is it? Is it a substance or is it something else? I think the best definition is "Energy is." In quantum physics the "energy substance" is called particles. The interesting thing about particles is that they can take any form and any route. They are completely random. Until they are observed or thought about. When they are observed or thought about, they take the form or the route that is expected. This has been proven in the *Feynman Double-Slit Experiment* and, later, it was proven that distance from the one who thinks about it to where the experiment takes place is irrelevant. Our thoughts affect how the particles behave, wherever we are—and whenever it is.

The first time I read that it was like an avalanche in my brain. My introduction to this field was through studying the Law of Attraction. I listened to *The Secret of Deliberate Creation* by Dr. Robert Anthony. Then I read *The Grand Design*, a book by Stephen Hawking et al, where the authors say that the Universe is governed by laws, and that these laws of the Universe determine the probabilities of various outcomes rather than certainty of a given outcome. To me, this means that we can use the Universal laws to our advantage, and everything is possible. Everything is possible. Meaning we can have the life we want if we use our energy in accordance with the Universal laws.

I am not going to dig more into this. As you know I am not a physical scientist, but I wanted to share this with you so that you understand that what I tell you in this book is not "quacks physics." It is real physics and you can use this to create the life you want. Unless you think that humans are not a part of the Universe, or that we are so special that Universal laws do not apply to you. Then you should probably put this book down and walk away. It's okay if you are not an immediate believer. That doesn't mean that the laws of the Universe do not affect you simply because you do not believe. Imagine if we had to learn about gravity for it to affect us; those who were not taught about gravity would simply disappear into space. Luckily this is not like that. The laws of the Universe are like that. They exist and impact us, whether we know it or not. Or believe it or not.

Going back to the last sentence in the definition: *energy is just the force that causes things to move.* By using your thoughts—since they are energy—you actually cause things around you to move. You are the cause, and what happens around you is the effect of your thoughts. We are part of the Universe (I assume we all agree on that), so let us take a look at what laws govern the Universe.

Chapter Eight

Seven Laws of The Universe You Can Use to Live the Life You Really Want.

There are seven fundamental laws in the Universe that we can use to our advantage to reach our goals. The Universe is made of energy. We are energy. Our thoughts are energy. We use the cause and effect to create the life we really want.

Understanding how the Universe works is the fastest and easiest way to be daring and to be different to create the life you really want.

Many people are ignorant when it comes to these laws. To be honest, I had not heard about them until I started studying this material either. We can say there are three reasons for this ignorance: You have not heard about them. You have heard about them but do not believe in them. Or you have heard about them and are not applying them.

Today, it is kind of strange to me that these laws and how they can be used to our advantage is not well known, but I think it comes from the programming we have been taught since we were small kids. We are taught to be rational humans—a part in the big machinery of society. As we know by now, we are energy and an important part of the Universe, whatever we like to think about, and these seven laws can be used to our advantage to create the life we really want to live.

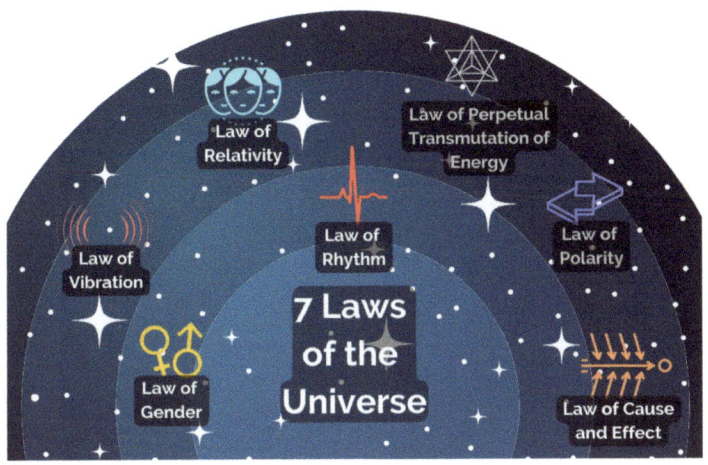

1. The Law of Vibration

The *Law of Vibration* decrees that everything moves, or vibrates, nothing rests. Everything ever created, from the smallest quantum particle (a "quark") to the largest skyscraper, is in a constant state of energetic motion. We know that energy is, and that energy never disappears—it only changes form.

The thoughts you think and get emotionally involved with are in control of the VIBRATION you are in. Feeling is conscious awareness of vibration.

From physics, we know that like energy attracts like energy. We know that opposites are pushed away. That is the principle of magnets. And it is the *Law of Attraction*: like energy attracts like energy. Your thoughts are energy that creates feelings. Feelings are waves of energy. And feelings affect your actions—which also are energy. That is why we can say that we become what we think.

Everything you want exists in two states:

- The thing you want.

- Lack of the thing you want.

And in between these two are all your emotions related to what you want. If your focus and feelings are on the lack of the thing you want, you will never get it. You cannot listen to your favorite FM station if you are on the AM band. You are on the wrong frequency. The *Law of Attraction* says that you attract what you feel.

It is like trying a new dress and thinking, "I can never have this." Then, you will never buy it because you feel you are not worthy of it. But if you focus on how amazing you will feel in this dress when you have it, you are into the spirit of it, then it will be yours when you are ready for it. You cannot have what you want from the emotional state of not having it.

When you understand the *Law of Vibration* and the *Law of Attraction*, instead of allowing the outside world to dictate what you think and how you feel inside, you start to live from the inside out by choosing and focusing on thoughts that align with what you want. This causes changes in your feelings (and vibrations) to attract and create the results you seek in life. The most powerful part of this is that you eliminate the possibility of getting what you do not want—because the Universe gives you what you feel. If you only think about what you want, you eliminate the negative outcome part of the equation.

Think about how you want to live. Think about what you really want and get into the feeling of having what you really want. First you feel it—then you get it. By focusing on what you want, you eliminate the possibility of getting what you do not want, and you increase the probability of getting what you want many times. We become what we think about.

2. The Law of Perpetual Transmutation of Energy

Perpetual means constant movement forever. It never stops.

This law explains that everything in the Universe that we can see, hear, smell, taste, or touch, together with our emotions, is the manifestation of energy in different forms—or frequencies. All frequencies are connected; there is a constant flow of an unlimited number of frequencies. Those of us who have tuned a FM/AM radio will understand that there is a flow of frequencies when we tune for a station.

Energy is in a constant state of transmission and transmutation. Energy is the cause and effect of itself and can be neither created nor destroyed. Energy is.

The *Law of Perpetual Transmutation of Energy* says that energy is always moving in and out of physical form. Rain starts with water being heated up; it moves up to the sky as moisture, creates clouds, is cooled down, and comes back to earth as rain—over and over again. It is a perpetual process.

We know that our thoughts are energy, and any idea or image that is held in the mind and emphasized has to move into its physical form because the emotions are expressed through the body as energetic feelings. Your feelings make you take action, and actions create the results.

3. The Law of Rhythm

The *Law of Rhythm* embodies the truth that everything is moving to and from, flowing in and out, swinging backward and forward. It shows us that there is always a reaction to every action.

This law governs everything from the movement of planets to what happens in your body. A lot of economics also say that an economy has rhythm and follows waves. The law can be observed in the rising and setting of the sun and moon, ebb and flow of the tides, coming and going of the seasons, and every human's hormone cycle.

Life is lived in contrasts, so you are not going to feel good all of the time; no one does. If you did, you wouldn't even know it. The low feelings are what permit you to enjoy the high feelings. When you are in a downswing, know the swing will change and things will get better. Good times are coming—choose to think of them and meet yourself with love and empathy, not anger. As soon as you realize you are in a downswing, it will change upwards.

There are two ways you can use this law to your advantage. The first is to know that there will be a better day, soon, when the "tide turns." The other way is to be aware of your rhythm, and then catch yourself on a low day and tell yourself to be more energetic and use your will to go through the day with a positive attitude.

All humans have their cycles. If you accept the idea that you can control your energy through your thinking, try to use the power of your mind to change how you feel. I am pretty sure you will be surprised if you practice this. A trick I use is to think about something I want for twenty seconds.

4. The Law of Relativity

To the Universe there is no small or big. Everything is energy—and it takes all possible forms. We think that big is big, but that is only true for our own perception and expectations.

In the study of this law, we find that all things are relative, including all laws. All laws are related to each other and correspond with each other. Every law must be in harmony, agreement, and correspond with each other.

For example, all rates of vibration are either high or low, only by comparison with those above or below them. All sizes are relative too. When I started my journey of creating the life I really want, I often wondered how good can one actually feel—and I do not know. I only know that I feel so much better than before—and that is just great.

Recognize that everyone does something better than you and, likewise, you do something better than every person you meet. We have no right to judge others, and why should we bother? Do not compare yourself with others. You are you—and there is a place for you. To judge yourself against what others do is to use the law against yourself. Instead, make a habit of using this law to your benefit—to heighten your self-esteem. You will then become aware of how special you are in the light of truth.

My sister and I always watched Pippi Longstocking on TV. I loved when she said, "I have never done that before, so I know I can do it."

Maybe you do not master it today—but practice always makes masters.

5. The Law of Polarity

The *Law of Polarity* decrees everything in the Universe has its opposite: hot/cold, good/bad, inside/outside. You have a right and left side to your body, a front and back. Every up has a down, and every down has an up.

The *Law of Polarity* not only states that everything has an opposite—it is equal and opposite. If it were three feet from the floor up on to the table, it would be three feet from the table down to the floor; it could not be any other way.

This law is so powerful; use it to your advantage. This is where you develop your perception—to always look for the good in everything around you—to see both sides of a person, situation, or circumstance. You will be empowered and inspired.

Using the *Law of Polarity* will help you move forward in the direction of the life you really want, because you will realize that everything in your life "just is" and you make it negative or positive by how you choose to think about the situation. It is your choices, not your circumstances, that will create the life you so desire.

There is an enormous power in being neutral and to look for the possibility in everything that happens. And since perception, and thereby context, is subjective, everything that is a threat is also a possibility. "This is so bad it has to be really good."

6. The Law of Gender

The *Law of Gender* is the creative law. This law decrees that everything in nature is both male and female. Both are required for life to exist.

Without the dual principle of male and female in all things, there could not be a difference of potential or energy. Life is lived in contrast—and change is contrast. All new things merely result in the changing of something that was into something else that now is.

We experience both masculine and feminine energy, which is known as the creative process. Creativity is a result of wanting something else, something new, something different. Both men and women have a masculine pole and a feminine pole, and the strength of each pole varies with, among other things, our personality, our experiences, and our DNA.

Consciousness (everything that we think, desire, and love—all that we believe is true and untrue) is the masculine energy, whereas the life force that brings form to the thought in physical reality is the feminine energy.

The *Law of Gender* decrees that all seeds have an incubation period before they manifest in the physical world. Ideas are spiritual seeds which turn into thoughts that make you feel and then move you into action. When you choose a goal, or build the image in your mind, a definite period of time must lapse before that image manifests in physical results. The mental challenge is that we do not know how much time it will take—and that is the biggest challenge. We want it to happen *now*, so we start to doubt—and doubt is poison to the creative process.

The purpose of having goals is the journey to the goal. It is who we become on our way to the goal that is the true meaning. We become who we want to be, and we live the life we really desire on the way to the goal. We are on our way to new goals and desires through our lives. We are never done. It is a perpetual process. We want something, so we change, and we get what we want. Then we launch new wants, and we change again, and again, and again.

For anything to grow it requires energy; plants require sun, for example. Our thoughts and ideas grow on the energy we give them through our thinking. Remember, as Andrew Carnegie said, "Any idea that is held in the mind, that is emphasized... will at once begin to clothe itself." The beauty is that we can speed the process up. We can go faster. We can develop ourselves more. The more we focus on the idea, the faster it happens. The concentration of thought relative to an idea increases more energy on that idea, bringing it more quickly into manifestation. The more we think about it, the more we want it, and the more actions we take.

7. The Law of Cause and Effect

Many say this is "the Law of Laws," and I tend to agree because we can really create the life we really want when we understand that we are the cause of everything that happens around us. This law states that whatever you send into the Universe comes back. Action and reaction are equal and opposite.

To repeat what Bob Proctor told many of his clients and me, "You have only one problem in life, and that is you. And you have only one solution in life, and that is you." If you continue to do what you do, you will have no change. So you have to change you (the cause) to change your life (the effect).

Everything in the entire Universe happens according to law—there is no such thing as chance. Every effect must have a cause, and in turn, that cause must have an effect. Thus, we have the never-ending cycle of cause and effect.

And here is the most important point, which is directly related to the Stick Person described earlier: Since our thoughts and feelings are energy, the life around us is an effect of what we think and feel. To use this law to our advantage and create the life we really want, we need to start thinking about what we want to have and feel the joy of having it.

Most people think more about what they *do not* want than what they want and feel the disappointment of not having it. This law tells us why it is no surprise when they end up getting exactly what they do not want.

Summary of the Seven Laws and The Butterfly Effect

These seven laws are all present—and they apply to your life and my life. The knowledge of them is a treasure for creating what you truly desire. Use these laws to your advantage to create what you truly want. What you think affects what you feel. What you feel affects your actions. And your actions create the life you want.

I know this can be overwhelming. My first thought when I realized this was that I had been an idiot for many years. There are so many things I could have done differently that cannot be undone. What has been has been.

I can only affect this exact moment in life. But when I realized I was so happy with being where I was in that moment, and that all my successes and failures had taken me to this point in life, my heart was filled with gratitude for being here.

When I started looking back to connect the dots, I realized that I had done some things the correct way, and that explained some of my successes. In business I have always been extremely goal oriented. We never made a strategy without first defining the goals. In business, that process is logical to me. We have to know where to go to know what to do. All we did was always linked to the goals we had. We had many successes, and when we failed in business it was because we lost focus and belief in our goals.

The "Eureka moment" for me was when I connected the dots that I can do the same thing in my life. My ideas are my goals. My goals give me new thoughts of how to achieve what I want (that is strategy), and my thoughts lead to the things I do (that is goal achieving activities).

Over time, my understanding of who I am and what I truly want increased. My trust in myself also increased. I started focusing on what I truly want to do and focused less and less on what I think others expect me to do. Step by step, I realized my true heart desires and, step by step, I changed my life. I started to be a deliberate creator. It was not like snapping my fingers, and there I was—happy, healthy, and wealthy with all I wanted. It was a constant move in the direction of my goals—two steps forward, one step back. Two steps to one side, oops wrong way, let me try the other way. Daring to try new things, go out of my comfort zone, follow my intuition, and challenge myself. Sometimes it feels like failing forward, though I never give up.

To be honest, I do not like so much the person I was before anymore. I do not like being angry. I do not like thinking, "Who the fuck do you think you are?" It is not an alternative to go back to being the person I was. I have changed and become a better version of me. I like to control my thinking, to focus on what I want. I like to be happy, to feel good, and to wonder about how things are. I like to write books (even though my editors drive me crazy sometimes, I love that they stretch my thinking). And I love to see how far I can go in this life. It is the understanding of the Universe and my thinking that is the key. It feels like I have upgraded myself from Christer 1.0 to Christer 2.0, and I do not want to downgrade myself to

1.0. I only want to upgrade to Christer 3.0. I want to grow and develop because that is so full of joy and freedom. Sometimes when we feel the Universe plays with us, my wife and I look at each other and say "What a life. What a great life."

We can only change one step at a time, based on where we are in each moment. It is a step-by-step process. We often say it is the journey that is the goal, not the goal itself. But how do you know that you do enough? Here is another physical effect that will give you trust and peace of mind in that the small steps you take every day in the direction of what you want are enough.

The *Butterfly Effect*

Many have heard about the *Butterfly Effect*, maybe from the movie or the saying that a butterfly in Brazil will affect the North Pole. That picture did not give me rest, so I looked it up. It is actually a mathematical effect derived from the first studies of meteorology. At the time they started developing methods for predicting weather for several days and weeks, they had limited computer capacity. They started with six decimals on all observations, but that took too much time to process so they changed to three decimals. For most of us it does not matter if it is 0.506 or 0.506487. But that three-digit change gave dramatically different prediction precision in the weather models they developed. *What could cause that?*

When working with weather, meteorologists work with the whole atmosphere as a system, and it's a pretty big system. But even a small change resulted in big effects. That is how we can use the *Butterfly Effect* to our advantage. We are working with the entire Universe as a system. So it takes very small changes in the beginning to get it right at the end. Fifteen percent correct at the beginning will give you eighty-five percent right at the end, given that you are consistent.

A small change in your consciousness and thinking—starting today—will change your life. It is a mathematical fact.

Action Steps

1. Write down how you can use these Seven Laws of the Universe to your advantage every day:

    ◦ Law of Vibration and Law of Attraction: What can you do to vibrate and attract what you desire?

- Law of Polarity: Based on what you know about your personality, that perception is individual and everything that is really bad is also really good, find at least three things in your life you can change—today—from unwanted to wanted. Use your imagination and think, "What would Christer think about this?"

- Law of Perpetual Transmutation of Energy: Your thoughts are energy. How can you use your thinking to get less of what you do not want and more of what you do want?

- Law of Gender. What can you do every day to have more discipline and more focus on the thoughts you like?

- Law of Rhythm: Which rhythms in nature affect your life? Is it more than your body's natural hormone rhythm? Are there any rhythms you can use to your advantage?

- Law of Relativity: Everything is energy. There

is no big or small. There is no "much or little." Everything is seen through your perception, and perception is individual. Everything just is, and all is defined by your perception. Are your dreams, wishes, or goals worthy of you?

- Law of Cause and Effect: Are you the cause in your life, or are you the effect of what happens around you? What can you do to be the cause in your life and create more of what you want?

All changes start with an effort. Then we need to practice every day to be great. What small, permanent changes can you make today to use the *Butterfly Effect* to your advantage in creating more of what you want?

Where Are You?

Steve Jobs said, "You can't connect the dots looking forward; you can only connect them looking backwards. So you have to trust that the dots will somehow connect in your future."

The life you have today is a result of everything you have thought. You are a result of your thinking so far. What you think you can and what you think you cannot. You think – feel – act according to your ideas, and your ideas create your life. Especially your ideas about yourself.

This was an eye opener to me; it made me look backwards to see my life in retrospect. *What was I thinking when I failed? What was I thinking when I had success? Was there a difference in my thoughts, feelings, and actions at different times?*

Oh yes, there was—big differences actually. I discovered that when I had success, I had clearly defined goals, was focused on them, and disciplined. I had people around me who were better than me in many areas, and we shared the same goals. I developed an attitude like, "It is what it is. Just do it. It will be great." I was into the spirit of my goals. And we were into the spirit of our company goals.

The times I failed, I lost focus on our company goals. We were in doubt if we could do it, or if this was the right way for us. We lost the spirit of our goal. It is my job as a manager of a company to be into the spirit of our goals, and make the organization into the spirit of our company goals. One of my mistakes was to try to stay the same instead of changing. I was enslaved by daily trivia optimizing the company instead of seeing the big picture, and starting to change. I should have stood up more clearly and said, "I do not believe in this path." The second error I made was to stay too long in my jobs. I was too stable and loyal. I should have found a new job when I was bored. And as a Choleric, I was easily bored. Now I realize that I was held back by the fear of losing what I had: status, financial freedom, and more. Everything looked good from outside, but not in my heart. And when you are not into the spirit of it, you fail. And spirit is in your heart.

The more aware I get, the more often I look backwards to connect the dots and see if I am on the right path. I look at my dominant thoughts to see where my focus is. I look at my results from a neutral perspective. I borrow my mentors' perception by asking myself what they would do in my situation. I evaluate if what I do is on the right path to my goals. I always want more, faster. A challenge for me is to accept the *Law of Gender,* that I do not know when things will materialize. As a Choleric, I always think more action solves everything. But sometimes I just need to sit down, focus on my true desires, let time work for me, and have faith that things always work out for me. If you are a Melancholy or Phlegmatic, do not take this as proof you can think into results only. It is thinking *and* acting that gives results.

My faith grows stronger and stronger every day. But doubt tends to slip into my mind. I know that is the "old me" trying to tell me that I am not good enough, or that it is not possible to do what I want, or I start to wonder what others think about me. I have to admit I had much more doubt before I became a deliberate creator. The more I work according to the Laws of the Universe, the more focused I become on my deliberate creation, the less doubt I get. I know I am on the right path. I assume that I will get what I want. I have accepted the idea as true or as certain to happen, without proof.

Your ideas are a result of your personality and your programming. Ninety-five percent of our daily actions are automatic—they are habits. They are programs in our subconscious mind. We call the program behind our habits, "paradigms." Most of your paradigms are good for you, but some are really bad.

Many paradigms are created at a young age. Before we are seven-years-old there are no boundaries between the conscious mind and the unconscious mind. So everything that happens affects our emotions immediately—and our mind has a fantastic ability to connect things so we remember what caused the feeling and, voila, we have a paradigm programmed in our mind! We now know that it is all about our perception, but when we are unaware of that, we are easily programmed. That is why it is so important to develop our perception—because this gives us an open mind. Use the *Law of Polarity* to challenge your perception: This is so bad it has to be so good.

If you are 100% happy and content with what you have and how your life is today, and you think you can have it like this the rest of your life without change, then continue as you are. More of the same gives more of the same. The challenge you can face is when everything else around you changes. As I learned when I was a young product manager in Nestlé:

"We constantly have to change to stay the same." This is because the world around us changes all the time. There is no, "stop the world, I am not ready yet," function in life

BE DARING. BE DIFFERENT.

If you want a change in your life, you have to change your paradigms. You must break the old habits and create new ones. That is the only way you can change your thinking, which changes your feelings, which changes your actions. Your want is the seed to your change.

CHRISTER JOHNSEN

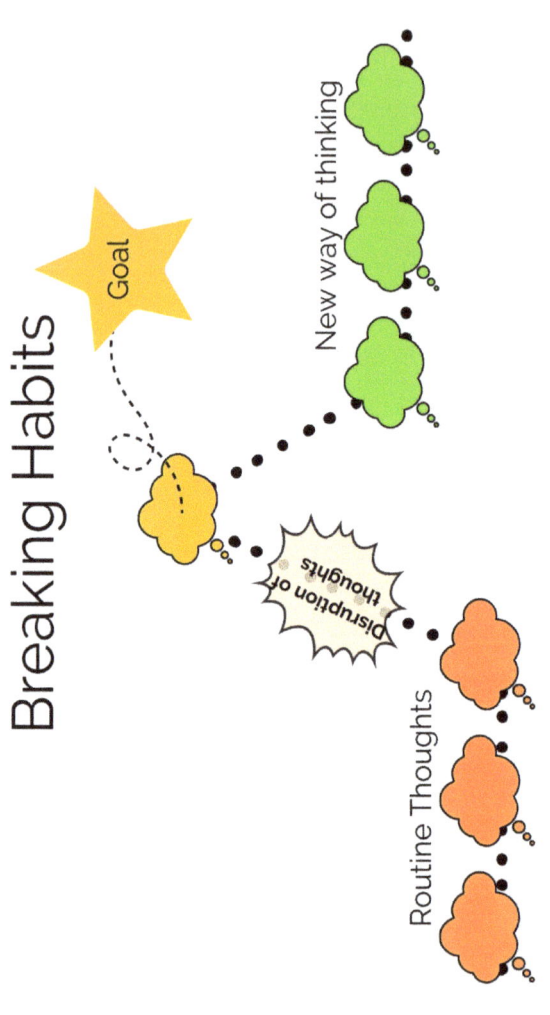

Chapter Nine

Self-Image

The key element and cause to what you have in your life is your self-image. The Oxford Dictionary defines it as, "the idea one has of one's abilities, appearance, and personality." Let us dig into this backwards.

Your idea about your personality—*Who am I and why am I like that?*—goes back to the four personality types described earlier. They can give you a good grip on who you are and why you behave and think like you do. We all have all four of them in us, but it is the dominant one and the second dominant type that matter most. Most of your personality is genetic, and that is given to you through generations. Not many people are consciously aware of their personality, although it is very enlightening to be aware of it. Especially when we know this so well that we start to see other people for who they truly are—only then can we truly understand them, and ourselves. Many of my clients have had an eye-opener when they understand their partner, and why they chose him or her, and what they love(d) about their partner.

Your appearance is how you look and how you think others view your look. What others think is not important! If you wonder what others think about you—well, they don't. Others are just like you and me; we mostly think about ourselves. How you look is a choice, and an important one. Maybe the fastest way to change your self-image is to change the way you look. Try to replace your business-style suit with a cockscomb hairstyle, wear a black leather jacket with pins, tight black jeans, and black boots. And see how that changes what you think and feel about yourself. What you can do and cannot do. It might be a right step for you, if that is what you really want. If not, just use your imagination and paint the picture of yourself in your mind.

The last element in the definition is your abilities. To me, that means mental abilities, not my physical abilities. What you think you can do. And what you think you cannot do. The latter is at least as important as the first one. This is where a bunch of your paradigms kick in, and where the biggest potential for personal growth and development lies. This is where interesting concepts like shame, worthiness, self-esteem, trauma, excuses, self-talk, etc., come in.

I was bullied for many years at school, which has been one of my most effective motivations. I want to be a winner. I want to show the world that I am better than those who bullied me. But this started to change when I was around forty-years-old when I realized that my anger was not doing me well. I reached a lot of goals, but I was not happy. I tried more of the same, and I got more of the same. I reached more goals—and was still unhappy. When I now look back at this, I remember exactly when I changed.

A friend of mine is an international certified coach. Over a cup of tea while discussing the Universe, the meaning of life, and personalities, she told me my personality, in the system she uses in her coaching, was "anger driven." It was like putting a needle in a balloon. Pssssssssssssssssssssss—a big burden was released from my shoulders and my stomach. I cannot say all of my anger was gone but it opened new doors for me, and I will always be grateful that she shared her insight with me. It was a life-changing moment, an emotional impact. I realized I did not want to be angry anymore.

> I realized I had to stop saying, "Who the fuck do you think you are?" to everyone I disagreed with. Instead, I started to say, "You are interesting—I wonder where you come from and why you think differently from me. This is interesting." That kicked off my new path in life.

Where Do You Want to Go? What Do You Want?

When I meet potential new clients, I always ask them what they want. Some are very clear in their response. To many, however, that is not an easy question to answer. Most people live their life as they think they are expected to—they perform their daily trivia so well that they ultimately become enslaved by it. How many hours do you spend on social media or in front of a TV every day? Often, it can be almost scary to think outside the "what you think is expected from you" box. We are programmed to think that it is best not to change. But that is not possible. We cannot stop our brain from working. If you think about nothing, you think about thinking nothing. There is no pause in this life, so why not make it as good as possible? How far can you go in this life?

Last year, I decided that my next thirty years will be my best, and that every year will be better than the last one. I want this life to be my greatest life. I accepted the idea that I will go as far as I can go. That is my choice—no one can take that from me. You, too, can make that choice yours.

Most people I meet as a mentor know that they want something else. Something more.

What if you can have anything you imagine? What do you imagine? What is your dream life? What words give you a blossoming heart and dreamy eyes? Freedom? Helping others? Effortless financial freedom? To work with what you really love? To share your life with the ones who loves you as much as you love them? To sail around the world alone? To be healthy? To have a fantastic career? To be a rock star? To be a world-known bestselling author? To fill the Sydney Opera house with a live event? To have all the peace of mind you want to have? To be world champion in horse riding? To be an Olympic champion in swimming?

There are no limits to what people want. The biggest challenge is to dare to think and say to yourself what you really want, and to accept the idea that you can have anything you truly desire. Accept that idea, and your life will start to change.

All goals start with a feeling of wanting something else than what we have today. This feeling of dissatisfaction is a great motivation for change, and to set a goal.

For almost ten years I had a goal of sailing around the world. This goal was so strong that when I met my wife, I told her that if she wanted to be with me, she had to join me sailing around the world. She is a wonderful woman, and she said OK in a second (she has a good dose of Choleric too). In my mind I had this beautiful picture of me standing on my boat—leaving home port—setting course for the open ocean. And I wanted to do it now! The compromise I made with my wife was to wait a few years until she could join me. This was one of the larger tests of my patience. I was in eyesight of my goal—I could leave now and do it. I could be the image I had imagined in my mind for ten years; the picture that changed my life and would give me my need for freedom back.

Many say there is a reason why things happen, we just do not see it yet. To me, this was a complete mental stretch. I got even more stuck into life, and more eager to accomplish my goal. I felt like I was treading water, barely able to breathe. I felt like a tiger in a cage, walking from side to side with a strong need to get out and stretch my legs. I felt like running on half machine because I had so much more inside me. So much more potential. So much more talent that I wanted to express. And I had to slow down. All this created an enormous desire for change. Like a rocket of desire for change inside me, I wanted more from this life. Bored by the daily trivia, I was also not easy to live with.

Then the world closed down in 2020—and everything changed. The change was inside me. I knew we could sail around the world. We had done everything to prepare for our new life, all that was left was to just do it. But the goal had lost its spirit in me. Thinking about it did not bring a big smile to my face anymore. I did not feel bad about that, however, because a new, bigger idea had come to my mind, one that was expanding every day. This new idea turned into a new goal; a seed that was sown many years ago was starting to sprout. The lockdowns took me out of slavery of my daily trivia; I had time to think, reflect, and feel that I wanted something more, something else.

Giving up sailing and exploring was out of the question. The new idea was to help others all over the world to live their full life too. Where I see people as they are, and how amazing they can be when they understand and accept to be deliberate creators. The new idea was to have the freedom I need, and at the same time, help others all over the world. To travel where we want when we want. To combine sailing with helping others to live their fullest life. A better, more fulfilling way to do what I love.

I was ready for the next step. I was ready to really challenge myself. To set a big, hairy goal I had no idea how to reach. A goal that makes me sparkle with energy every day. So I opened the door to the cage and let the tiger out. My machine was revving up, and I did a really smart move—I found a great mentor. My instruction to him was to kick me out of my daily trivia and make me move fast. And he did.

Action Steps

1. What is your self-image? What do you tell yourself you can do or cannot do? What are you really good at, what can you improve? Do you love yourself?

2. Describe how far you can go when you do what you truly want?

3. What is your true heart's desire—what do you really want to do?

4. If you have a strong desire for change, find a mentor who knows how to help you do it.

Chapter Ten

Set Goals

There is only one valid reason for setting a goal: "I want it!"

Do not argue with anyone, including yourself, about your goals. Some will think you are nuts. Sometimes you *feel* nuts. Some will envy you. Others will just not understand. They see the world through their own looking glasses. The only thing that is important is that YOU WANT IT.

"In the absence of clearly defined goals, we become strangely loyal to performing daily trivia until ultimately we become enslaved by it," said Robert Heinlein. In order to create what we truly want, we have to realize we are stuck in daily trivia and routines, and we have to get out of them. The way out of daily trivia is to set clearly defined goals that you truly want.

There are three types of goals. I call them "A Goal," "B Goal," and "C Goal."

An "A Goal" is what you know you can reach, e.g., I want a new car. Most people have "A Goals."

A "B Goal" is what you think you can reach, like I want to sail around the world. I think I can do it and I have an idea of how I can do it.

A "C Goal" is a goal you really want to have or reach—but you have no idea *how* to reach it. I want to have a business that operates all over the world helping thousands, or be a successful author, or create an amazing amusement place for culture, or be an international film producer, pop star or successful CEO of a global company.

"A Goals" start with, "that would be nice." "B Goals" start with, "I wonder if I can," and "C Goals" start with a dream, a vision, an "imagine if I could do that."

The more thoughts and energy you give to your goals, the more your self-image changes. What was exciting before is not as exciting now. What gave you butterflies in the stomach some months ago does not resonate so well with you today. When you open up your perception and imagination, you think more about what you really want than what you think you can have. You accept the idea of having your goal without knowing how to get it. You see yourself as worthy of it. Your world is expanding.

Why this focus on goals? Why do we even need goals? Do you remember the Laws of Vibration and Attraction? Your thoughts are energy. Like energy attracts like energy. When you focus on what you want (your goal) you create order in your mind. It is like magnetizing steel. The steel is the same, but the electrons are all in the same direction. You magnetize your mind with your goals and use the Universal laws to your advantage, creating what you really want. As Bob Proctor said, "If you can keep it in your mind, you can hold it in your hand."

We become what we think about. What you think affects what you feel. What you feel affects what you do. And what you do creates your life. You create the *You* that you really want to be.

> The purpose of the goal is not to get what you want, it is who you become on your journey to the goal.

When you are in your goal, you think, "What is next?" And that is the beauty of this life—we can have what we really want, over and over again.

Action Steps

1. Write down how you really want to live. Do not think about how you can get there. Do not think about how likely it is. Do not think about what others think or might think. Just write down what you really want in life.

2. To find your goals, start writing down things you really like to do, what feels good when you do it, and what feels good when you think about it. If that is challenging, start writing a list of what you do not want. To some, that is a better start. I think

most of us are pretty clear about what we do not want. From that "do not want" list, start to look at the opposite, at what you do want.

Chapter Eleven

How Do I Get There? Be Daring. Be Different.

Now that you know what you want (or at least what you do not want), it is time to look at how you get what you want. And for many, this process is totally different than you may expect. It is a fun and inspiring journey. It is effortless. It is challenging in a different way than you might think. First of all, it is a mental activity.

Let us go back to Andrew Carnegie, "Any idea that is held in the mind, that is emphasized, that is either feared or revered, will immediately start to clothe itself in the most convenient and appropriate physical form available." Let us also repeat the physics in this. You are a power plant full of energy. Feeling is conscious awareness of vibration. Energy is vibration at different levels. Vibrations can be heard like words and music tones, seen as different colors of light etc., and felt like warm or cold water.

Vibrations are frequencies—and there are an unlimited number of frequencies. Everything has its own frequency. Your sadness has a lower frequency than your happiness. A piece of metal has its vibration. A stone has its vibration. A dead body has its vibration (otherwise it would not decay). Everything that exists has its own frequency. Your goals have their own frequency too. *What do you feel when you think about being in your goal?* That is your goal's frequency. Wow—that feels good! I smile every time I think about my goals, every time I am in my goals with my imagination.

Funnel of Limitation

Dr. Robert Anthony describes your perception of what is possible as a Funnel of Limitation.

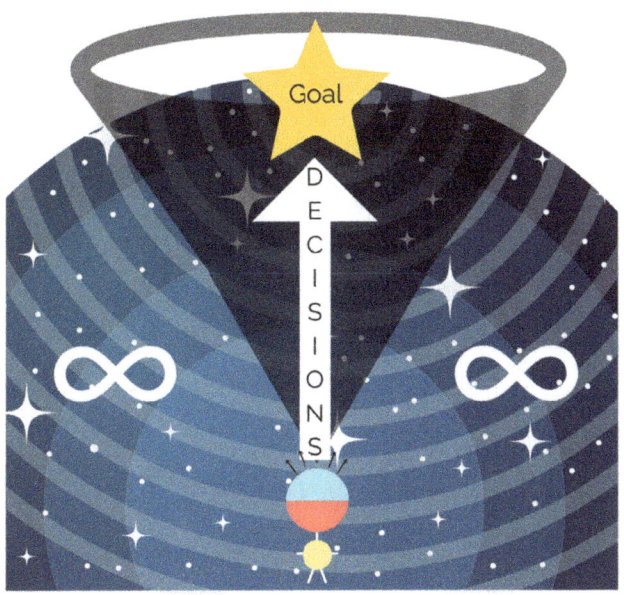

The outer frame here can be seen as the Universe—with its unlimited size and knowledge (the Universe is constantly expanding)—therefore the "unlimited" symbols on each side. The curved lines are frequencies, described in our world as feelings and things. The lines can also be seen as levels, or awareness, or frequencies. The star is your "C Goal." The arrow is your decision—this is what I want. And the Stick Person is you where you are today.

We have no idea how big the Universe is, and it is still expanding. I think about it as unlimited. Unlimited possibilities. Unlimited levels of awareness. Unlimited in terms of how far I can go. The only limit to me is what I can wrap my head around—that is limited by my imagination and perception. And that expands every day because I accept new ideas of what is possible all the time.

When we set a "C Goal," it is not important to know how to get there. The only thing that is important is that you want it and that you make the irrevocable decision: This is what I want. No matter what happens, I will never give up.

When President Kennedy wanted to send a man to the moon in the 1960s, he asked Dr. Wehrner von Braun, Chief of NASA, "What does it take to build a rocket that will carry a man to the Moon and bring him safely back to Earth?" von Braun knew that had never been done before. He knew they had to learn new things. He knew there were risks. His answer was, "The will to do it, Mr. President." That is all it takes for you too. Your will to do it.

BE DARING. BE DIFFERENT.

By focusing on the goal you will develop the skills, attitude, and awareness necessary to reach your goal. Your awareness will grow, and you will grow and change as a person. You will move up higher and higher in the Funnel of Limitation and see more and more possibilities. You broaden your mind and expand your awareness. You can see more possibilities, more resources, and so many more fun things to do.

> If you try to solve how to reach your goal before you take action, you will never reach your goal.

As you see—you are not at the frequency or the awareness where you have what you need to create a plan to reach the goal.

When you focus on *what* you want, not *how* to get it, you build an emotional momentum, and the Law of Attraction starts to work for you and not against you. You attract everything you need to reach the goal. You think and act like the person you want to be when you act like you are in your goal. You imagine yourself being there, and act how you think you will when you are there. Your actions do not have to be perfect as long as your intention is perfect. The *Butterfly Effect* works for you.

I like to compare a person's level of awareness and moving up in the Funnel of Limitation to what we view from different levels in a house. From the basement, you might see grass and light outside. From the ground floor, you can see the garden and sun. From the first floor, you can see more houses and the sky. From the second floor, you can see the neighborhood and the contour of a city. From the third floor, you can see the city, and from the roof, you can see the horizon and other cities. The higher up you get, the more possibilities you see, and you will feel better and better because you are reaching a higher frequency. With your imagination you can feel what you see from the roof, similar to seeing yourself in your goal. You move up in the funnel of limitation. You find more options for how to reach your goal and you see less limitations. As your awareness grows, your self image expands.

Funnel of Limitation

Of course, there can, and likely will, be setbacks and failures. It is our job to learn from them. We are failing forward and upwards in the funnel but, because you have made an irrevocable decision that, "This I will do," you continue with stronger and stronger persistence—and you grow into a new and better you.

If you feel it is right to set a time for when you want to reach the goal—be daring. I want to reach most of my goals no later than one year from the day they move from dream to goal. And if I do not reach them, I learn from that and set a new date. I never talk myself down. Instead, I focus on learning. *Who do I need to become to reach the goal? What self-image, attitude, discipline, and standard do I have when I am in my goal?* The Law of Gestation states that we do not know the incubation time for an idea—and so it is with a goal. I do not give up; I have accepted the idea of me in my goal and I have the will to do it.

Subjective Control

Do you direct your attention from within or from without?

There are so many things that go on around us all the time: social media, TV and print media, friends, family, work, training, etc. How is it possible to keep your focus on the goal and what you really want?

It is both easy to do and easy not to do, so it is a good idea to practice every day.

Dr. Robert Anthony calls it the "flip switch."

> When you are upset or affected by things around you that you do not like, choose the thought that makes you feel best in the moment.

That thought is most likely the picture you have in your mind of you in your goal. Thinking about that will give you a good feeling in your body—you raise your energy and frequency to the frequency of your goal. Do that over and over again. Every time you see that your feelings are controlled by something external, think about your goal. Observe how that affects you. Through practice and repetition, you develop a paradigm where you take control of your feelings. You reject thoughts that give you a feeling you do not want by replacing the thought with thinking about what you do want.

Another similar concept, based on the Stick Person figure, is called "touching lightly." This is to create a mental barrier between your conscious mind and your subconscious mind. When circumstances around you make you feel upset, afraid, not worthy, bad or sad, touch those things lightly. It is like playing a guitar; you have a firm grip on it, but you play the strings softly. Meaning you have a firm grip of your life, and do not let what happens around you affect your feelings in an unwanted way. You do not let those ideas come into your subconscious mind and either strengthen an unwanted paradigm or create a new unwanted paradigm. You say "No, that is not my thing. I reject that idea in my life." You protect your mind by focusing on what makes you feel good.

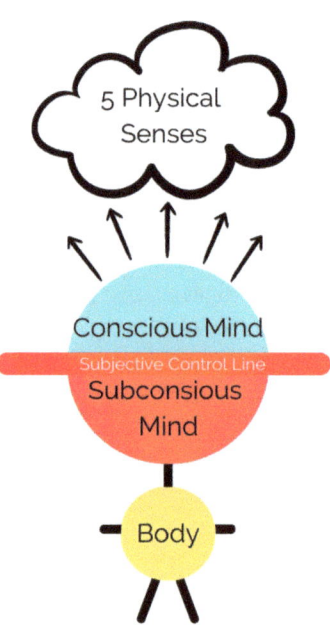

Reprogram Your Mind – Magnetize Your Mind to Your Success

Everyone has many paradigms and habits that control much of our day. Most of them serve us well. Some of them have served us well until now—but they need to change for you to reach your goals. The purpose of the goal is the creation of the *you* you must become on your way to the goal. The goal itself is a materialized proof of the journey you have been on.

There are two ways of changing a paradigm, but it starts with you accepting the idea that you want to change—that you want something else.

The first way is to create a strong emotional impact. I have mentioned two examples from my life in this book. The first was when I caught the falling knife that made me trust my intuition. Second was when my friend said that my personality is anger-driven. Both experiences had such an emotional impact on me that I know they changed my programming and paradigms. Life-changing events, like an accident or losing a dear friend, can also be big traumas.

The other way of changing a paradigm is by using affirmations and repetition. Through repetition we reprogram our brain—make new paths in our thinking—and, step by step, we reprogram our mind to believe what we tell ourselves. It can be seen as a way of self-hypnosis. In his book, *Think and Grow Rich*, Napoleon Hill calls it "autosuggestion." Through repetition, we impress our mind with new thoughts and ideas, and over time we believe them more and more. And when we believe in them, we get emotionally engaged in them.

"I am so happy and grateful now that I have all the peace of mind I want in life."

"I am so happy and grateful now that I receive more and more money with ease and from known and unknown sources."

"I am so happy and grateful now that I am a successful international author writing the best books in the world about IT and Artificial Intelligence."

Such affirmations must be mixed with positive emotions. Without positive emotions, nothing will happen and the more you repeat them, the better you will feel about them. What you think affects your feelings, your feelings affect your actions, and your actions create your life. We become what we think about.

Through life we have all experienced good and bad things. Some things we deeply regret or feel very bad about. There can be traumas or other circumstances that are difficult to deal with.

> To make a change in your life, you must realize that you can't undo what has been done. The only thing you can do is to change how they make you feel.

I know that can be easier said than done—but if you really want to change, you have to replace that old, negative energy with new, fresh energy. You have to let it go and replace it with good thoughts and feelings by focusing on your goal. Let history be history—let it go—and focus on what you want to have.

Faith

The truth will always resonate with us. What I write about in this book has been told for thousands of years. The Bible says, "Ask and you shall receive," and "Before you speak, I will hear you." There are many books and articles about the same subjects, but no other book puts all bits and pieces from personality to quantum physics, to math, to spirituality, to faith together like this book. It all boils down to faith and understanding. The recipe for having more of what you want is to understand the Universe from either a spiritual level or a physical level. Both ways work—as long as you believe in it, think about what you want, and take action.

Doubt is poison to all creative processes. Doubt will lower your feelings and vibrations. I say a hard NO to all doubt that comes to my mind. If you doubt if this works, borrow my faith. When I doubt, I borrow my mentor's faith.

We humans are so trained in the concept of "seeing is believing." We believe that things are possible when we see them. What a boring reality that must be without any dreams, imagination, and wonders. That is not the world I want to live in.

To me, faith is the ability to see the invisible, to believe in the incredible, and that is what enables believers to receive what the masses think is impossible.

> Faith is a choice. Do you believe it when you see it? Or do you see it when you believe it? Lack of evidence is not evidence of lack. We only see what happens in our consciousness. We do not see what happens outside our consciousness. Yet.

Deliberately Create the Life You Really Want

The human body is energy (in different forms). Our thoughts are energy and there are Universal laws that state that everything vibrates (everything is energy), and like energy attracts like energy. We can create the life we want. You have come a long way by reading this book, accepting the ideas I share with you, and doing the action steps in every chapter.

The next phase is to do it every day. It is actually easy to do. The challenge is that it is also easy not to do. To stay on track, I find great support in having a daily routine that I train myself to follow. I use my mental will to follow the routine every day to deliberately create my life.

I started looking backwards, thinking about the effects of doing what I have written about in this book, and I was amazed. Following this daily routine, I saw big changes in my life after one hundred days. After three hundred days, my life was completely changed. I had changed as a person. I now easily do what I used to be afraid of. I have new, wonderful people in my life. I am happier. I do what I love. I have the freedom I need. And we sail when we want, where we want. When I started the routine, I did not know I would write a book. I had never thought about being an author. Now I love writing, and I started writing this book on day "333" of following this routine.

These are four steps I use and recommend following:

1. Be grateful for what you have: This makes your thoughts go away from what you do not have. It raises your feelings and vibrations to a level where you are ready to look outside what you have today.

You are ready to set a goal. And you are ready to receive it. I am grateful for what I have and I am eager for more.

2. Start focusing on what you want: This is to set goals for what you really want in life. Think about what you want. Be emotionally engaged in your goal. Fall in love with it.

3. Reprogram your mind through affirmations and autosuggestions: Use the "flip switch" or "touching lightly" concepts to keep your thoughts, feelings, and vibrations on the level of your goal. Be persistent. Do not give up. Success is just around the next corner.

4. Think and act like the person you want to be: Think and act like *you in your goal*. Your actions do not have to be perfect, but your intentions of acting like that person must be perfect. You have to be into the spirit of your goal. You must act like you are the one you want to be. What would you do? Who would you team up with? What would you look like? Use your imagination to create this.

Acting is a crucial element in this. We cannot think life into our new life, we have to think *and* act. You have to take actions, make decisions, and step-by-step start the path towards your goal from the person you want to be when you are in the goal. Use your imagination to see how you will be in the goal—imagine how that feeling will be and act based on that.

Chapter Twelve

How To Do It: Create a Daily Ritual

For many years I have said, "We can sleep when we die." I have this sense of urgency that drives me, and it is a paradigm now to start the day early. My alarm goes off at 5am every morning because I do not have time to give away to bad habits. I have so much to do. I have a clear sense of urgency—I want to see how far I can go to help as many as possible. I see every day as day number one of the rest of my life. Every day is a step closer to my goal. Whatever I have or want, I can never get yesterday back—days gone are not for sale.

I spend about eight percent of my time awake focusing on my goals and taking the right steps for me to reach my goals. As an economist, I think that is the best investment I am ever going to make.

I start every morning like this:

- Write down at least ten things I am happy and grateful for.

- Write down ten-to-twenty "I am" statements to create the self-image I want to have. This is who I think I need to be to reach my goals (e.g., I am powerful, I do things right away, I am focused, I challenge my fears).

- Write my "C Goal" five times.

- I study one article or one chapter in a book that is relevant to my goal.

- I say my Goal Card out loud five times while looking into my eyes in a mirror.

- I meditate for ten-to-twenty minutes during the day. Meditation resets my mind. I often meditate in the morning.

- In my pocket, I carry a small card with my goals written on it. I always bring that with me. Every time I touch it, I think about my goals, see myself in the goals, and enjoy the rush of happiness it gives me. An alarm on my phone rings every three hours to remind me to spend two-to-three minutes reading my goal card. If I cannot read it, the alarm reminds me to think about my goals.

At the end of every day, I do a quick self-assessment:

- Have I leaned "into the spirit of my goal" today?

- I write down three-to-six wins, so I end the day with a good feeling.

- I write down three-to-six goal achieving actions I will do the next day—in present tense. That is my plan for the next day, and tomorrow I know what to do.

- I write my "C Goal" five times to repeat my goals.

It is through this repetition that I keep the idea of my goals in my mind and emphasize them. It is through repetition that my belief in achieving my goals grows into a desire to reach them. It is through repetition that I keep the goal my dominant thought during the day—and this keeps my feelings and emotions at a high frequency. It is through self-assessment that I evaluate my results and make sure I am on the right track. All these things are easy to do. And they are also easy not to do. That is where discipline comes in, and is why I have a daily ritual.

We can all be 1% better every day. 1% more focused on what we want. 1% more disciplined. 1% better at making decisions. 1% better at being grateful. Those who can do the math know that 1% each day is an enormous change over a year. $1.01^{365}=37.8$ times better. That is all it takes. Deliberately be 1% better every day, and your life will change a lot during a year.

Chapter Thirteen

Summary

The Universe is expanding constantly. That is because components have been gathered—particles are being attracted to each other—and that gives more energy. New platforms for ideas and wants are created. Through our wants, we are creators of our world, and our wants are expanding all the time. "Oh, I reached that goal! Let me see what more I can do."

As Thomas Troward so beautifully stated in his *The Dore Lectures on Mental Science*: "My mind is a center of Divine operation. The Divine operation is always for expansion and fuller expression, and this means the production of something beyond what has gone before, something entirely new, not included in the past experience, though proceeding out of it by an orderly sequence of growth. Therefore, since the Divine cannot change its inherent nature, it must operate in the same manner with me; consequently, in my own special world, of which I am the center, it will move forward to produce new conditions, always in advance of any that have gone before."

Go out and create your own life. Dream big. Focus on what you want. Use your higher faculties and the Laws of the Universe. Share this way of living with everyone who is ready for it. Be daring. Be different. Find your own way and create the successful life like you want it to be.

To your success!

The third emotional impact that changed my life: Thank you Bob Proctor. You will always be my inspiration. I will always be grateful for the gifts you gave me, and that you were the start of me being daring and different. Thank you!

Chapter Fourteen

Work With Me

What I Study

These are some of the books I study. There is a difference between reading and studying. When I study, I read a part every day for thirty days. Every time I read my perception changes, and I find new things.

Littauer, Florence, *Personality Plus for Couples* (Michigan: Revel, a division of Baker Publishing Group, 2001)

Hill, Napoleon, *Think and Grow Rich* (Connecticut: The Ralston Society, 1937)

Troward, Thomas, *The Dore Lectures of Mental Science - The Original Classic Edition from 1909* (USA: Start Publishing LLC, 2012)

Allen, James, *As a man thinketh* (Independently Published 2023)

Hawking, Stephen & Mlodinow, Leonard, *The Grand Design* (Great Britain: Bantam Press, 2010)

Anthony, Dr. Robert, *The Secret of Deliberate Creation: The secret to creating your life by design instead of by default.* (Audiobook: 2005)

You can also find more information about my mentoring and programs on my website:

www.christerjohnsen.com

Template for Your Daily Ritual

Here are some templates you can copy and use to create your own routines.

Goal Card

You can have one or several goals. Write all your goals in present tense. The goals shall be emotionally positive to you.

I am so happy and grateful now that I:

1.
2.
3.

Daily Ritual Form

Start every morning with:

- Write your goal by hand five times.

- Write down at least ten things you are happy and grateful for.

- Write down ten-to-twenty "I am" statements (e.g., I am powerful, I do things right away, I am focused, I challenge my fears)

- Say your goal card out loud five times while looking at yourself in the mirror.

Meditate for fifteen-to-twenty minutes during the day.

Always bring your goal card with you. Every time you touch it, think about your goals.

During the day:

Set an alarm on your phone that rings every three hours. Spend two-to-three minutes repeating your goal and your "I am" statements. Either read the goal card or listen to a recording you have on your phone.

At night:

- Write down three-to-six Daily Wins (Self-assessment: Have I leaned into the spirit of my goal today?)

- Write down three-to-six goal achieving actions you will do the next day in present tense.

- Write your goal card by hand.

- Say your goal card out loud five times while looking at yourself in the mirror.

"I Am" Statements

1_____
2_____
3_____
4_____
5_____
6_____

7_____

8_____

9_____

10_____

I am so happy and grateful now that:

1_____

2_____

3_____

4_____

5_____

6_____

7_____

8_____

9_____

10_____

Night ritual

Write down five daily wins of today:

1_____
2_____
3_____
4_____
5_____

Write down 3-6 goal-achieving activities you shall do the next day.

1_____
2_____
3_____
4_____
5_____

Acknowledgements

Thanks to my wife Elin for making our life so wonderful, and that we explore this amazing life together!

Thanks to my two editors Larissa Soehn and Ruth Fae for making this book even better than I thought was possible.

Thank you to Maria and Andreas for choosing me to be your father.

Thank you to my mentors. You have made me change. And this book is a result of that.

And thanks to all my clients for letting me help you and giving me all the joy and appreciation it is to share this wonderful journey with you all.

Author Bio

Mentor, International Speaker, Author, and Founder/CEO of christerjohnsen.com, Christer Johnsen is an explorer of life. His life motto, "How far can I go?" has taken him to a great international career. At twenty-nine-years-old he was CEO of his first company; at thirty-four, he was a successful CEO of an international group that operated in more than thirty countries. His motto has also taken him high up hiking mountains, deep down diving wrecks, caves, and reefs, and far away on his sailboat.

Christer has a genuine desire to help others be successful. After being bored and disillusioned in his corporate life, Christer's interest in helping other people showed him his new goal and path forward. Now working full time as Mentor and Coach, he helps people and organizations to set goals, become high performers, and reach their goals and desire to create the life they love. His programs are unique and, over time, have proven to be very successful for clients across the world. His first book, *Be Daring. Be Different.*, is a summary of the foundation of his programs and takes you through the process of creating the life you really want.

As an author, Christer has the unique ability to combine psychology, science, and knowledge about how the Universe works with simple and easy steps everyone can make to create more of what they really want. He likes to share his experiences from his own life to give his writing a personal touch.

A product of his work and writing, Christer is a true, deliberate creator of what he really wants in his life. Every day he lives what writes. He and his wife now live where they want, doing what they love. They have a house in Norway, a place in Asia, and they continue to explore the world on their beautiful sailboat.

Christer always appreciates the new people who come into his life, and he is happy to help you. Find out more about his mentoring programs and services, and books at:

www.christerjohnsen.com

CHRISTER JOHNSEN

www.ingramcontent.com/pod-product-compliance
Lightning Source LLC
Chambersburg PA
CBHW042115100526
44587CB00025B/4063